Pinterest Marketing

How to Use Pinterest for Business
Awesomeness

*(A Complate Step by Step Beginner's Guide to
Pinterest Marketing)*

Alberta White

Published By **Bengion Cosalas**

Alberta White

Pinterest Marketing: How to Use Pinterest for Business Awesomeness (A Complate Step by Step Beginner's Guide to Pinterest Marketing)

ISBN   978-1-998901-17-3

Legal & Disclaimer

The information contained in this ebook is not designed to replace or take the place of any form of medicine or professional medical advice. The information in this ebook has been provided for educational & entertainment purposes only.

The information contained in this book has been compiled from sources deemed reliable, and it is accurate to the best of the Author's knowledge; however, the Author cannot guarantee its accuracy and validity and cannot be held liable for any errors or omissions. Changes are periodically made to this book. You must consult your doctor or get professional medical advice before using any of the suggested remedies, techniques, or information in this book.

Table Of Contents

Chapter 1: What Is The Reason Of Pinterest?

Since its inception in 2009, Ana White's blog has provided her with a platform thru which she can be capable of percentage her enthusiasm for woodworking with others. In the start, the internet site modified into created as a way for her to percentage furniture-building designs with others, at the aspect of the beautiful mattress body she constructed for her own domestic. Almost every day, she updated her weblog with photographs and thoughts for contemporary day crafts. She moreover suggested recollections approximately her family's lifestyles in a small town in rural Alaska's indoors.

In the modern-day, ordinary with White, his blog has around three million net web page perspectives every month. To the factor, despite the fact that the sheer quantity of web page traffic may be startling in and of itself, the supply of that visitors can be an lousy lot extra so.

Pinterest now not handiest serves as White's most well-known deliver of internet page site site visitors, but it moreover gives her internet site 6,000 new internet site site visitors each day. It took definitely years for one Alaska mom's weblog to start producing enough advertising earnings to useful resource her complete own family.

White's weblog is a remarkable wholesome for the platform afforded via Pinterest, and she or he or he or he has loads to mention about it. It appears as despite the fact that her furnishings designs and domestic pictures are spreading like wildfire at the photo-sharing net site, and those are sharing her posts with their pals as they plan their private obligations within the destiny, as she describes. Follow her on Instagram, in which she goes via way of the manipulate to examine more about her pinning technique.

As a prevent cease end result, White has received incredible ranges of notoriety because of her weblog and Pinterest account. Her designs and products are likewise of high exceptional. She, but, is sharing her tale with you no longer handiest to introduce you to a lovely artist, but moreover to offer you with a glimpse of what is feasible on the equal time as using Pinterest. People use Pinterest to connect to distinctive human beings. If you do right and green Pinterest advertising, this will be a exceptional way to get oldsters which might be interested in your enterprise to come in your internet internet site on-line and grow to be your lovers and fans, no matter what you do within the future.

The Seductive Power of Pinterest

Apparently, Ben Silbermann, one of the co-founders of Pinterest, was a infant prodigy who amassed glass cases complete of insects and stamps at the same time as he became a little one. Pinterest become based due to this collector's mind-set, which served because the incentive for its inception. In slight of the truth that the act of accumulating is good sized, Silbermann set out to increase an internet platform that could make the act of online gathering—similarly to the sharing of those collections—as clean and charming as possible. We may additionally probable characteristic a huge a part of our dependancy to Pinterest to the fact that it lets in us to specific and satisfy our inner collector in a fun and innovative way.

According to Dr. Christopher Long, a professor of purchaser psychology at Ouachita Baptist University, the forums are defined as follows through the usage of Dr. Christopher Long, in keeping with his facts: According to him, "Pinterest boards are much like the customers' non-public happiness collages.It does not don't forget if it's far a discipline of cupcakes or a bare David Beckham; it is how they portray themselves that I recognize, desire, and convey who I am through their goods, "affords the author.

According to Chelsea Smith, a social media professional for Oreck, the enterprise's CEO requested that she set up a Pinterest account for the commercial organization company after he and his own family went on a vacation to

Mexico and located some aspect out of the regular. According to him, the lady people of his vacation organization have been "more worried with getting tans and ingesting margaritas" than they have been with getting tans and sipping margaritas. He stated that he wasn't really certain what the net net site changed into approximately, however he did point out that "this is vital" except. "We must get taking place this!" says the organization. As a final results, Smith had already installation a Pinterest account for the vacuum cleanser commercial enterprise employer and have been given permission to start making plans large Oreck Pinterest advertising and advertising and marketing campaigns.

Addictive? Yes. Oreck has made a notable marketing and advertising effort to sell its products. Absolutely.

Smart organizations have come to be greater famous with Pinboard, mainly now that it has established itself to be a strong deliver of internet website site visitors and leads for them.

Pinterest's target audience

You've in all likelihood heard via now that almost all of the cutting-edge-day Pinterest client base is made from lady people. While the right opportunities vary from check to have a have a look at, maximum professionals agree that spherical 60% of Pinterest users inside the United States are girl, with the majority of them being some of the a while of 25 and 34.

Despite this, there may be now not a few element basically woman-centric approximately the web page; it's far simply an photo-sharing service that permits human beings to build up their favored things from at some stage in the internet. The truth that Pinterest modified into particularly famous with a younger female demographic organization at its inception have grow to be a glad twist of destiny. However, due to the fact the net website on line maintains to expand, there's no purpose to count on that it will not moreover attraction to a big fashion of male customers. It's already starting to lure a huge range of male device enthusiasts and domestic improvement fanatics by using manner of the rating.

For example, Mike Street (@mikestreet), a social media strategist, continues a extraordinary series of male-pleasant pins on a Pinterest board he has dubbed "BroPin." Among the more than 800 pictures on his board—that is a collaborative university maintained by means of extra than 35 guys— are photographs of clothing, vehicles, era, and delicacies which might be uniquely appealing to men. Also on Pinterest, Ben Golder (@beng), a student of ecological architectural format from Barcelona with nearly 200,000 fans, curates forums on robots and shape which is probably geared at men.

Besides america, Pinterest has a developing client base in different areas of the globe, with a gender stability this is drastically one-of-a-kind from that visible inside the United States. For instance, Pinterest gets over hundred,000 specific visits every month from the United Kingdom, with guys making up the bulk of these customers' (56 percentage) visits to the net web site.

Consequently, do no longer consider all people who says Pinterest is only for ladies or that it's far simplest beneficial for advertising and marketing in ladies's-orientated corporations including weddings and fashion. But for now, allow's speak about how to utilize Pinterest for non-income and B2B businesses, similarly to a manner to apply it on your very very own non-public logo.

Be aware of the fact that Pinterest is a flexible, exquisite, and smooth-to-use platform that could offer big blessings to a massive variety of companies and customers.

So, what are the benefits of using Pinterest for advertising and marketing? Clever and a success agencies are the use of Pinterest a good manner to acquire new leads, enhance internet site on line website online site visitors to their websites, and communicate with their customers. Here are some examples:

If used properly, Pinterest may be a precious asset in your content material cloth marketing plan. When it comes to the internet, content cloth remains king, and Pinterest's visible material can be a treasured asset in rounding out any online advertising and advertising and marketing and advertising and advertising and marketing plan. It is possible to draw new clients and assemble strong connections with contemporary customers by using manner of publishing terrific cloth on blogs, social networking internet websites, and image-sharing internet websites together with Pinterest, amongst distinctive locations. And, in case your material is simply notable, those customers and fanatics can be greater than willing to unfold the phrase approximately your enterprise. What more have to you likely want?

Consumers' purchasing alternatives are being made primarily based on what they see on social media. According to a survey completed in January 2012 through the Massachusetts-primarily based completely advertising software program program corporation HubSpot, humans are 71% more likely to make a purchase while a product or service is usually

9

recommended via way of a pal thru social networking.Business proprietors who ensure their products are smooth to locate and advise on social media internet websites like Pinterest are clever, and they are trying this on their private.

Making your brand more human Because of Pinterest's visible nature, it is an exceptional tool for imparting customers (and ability clients) with a glimpse into the coronary heart of your organisation and what you want to offer.

What the business enterprise is all about Your pinboards will become more human the extra you permit your logo's character to shine thru, and your Pinterest effects will decorate due to your efforts to perform that.

It has the capability to feature a persistent deliver of motivation for you. No remember what industrial business enterprise you work in, speakme to others on Pinterest and browsing awesome fabric may be a wonderful supply of thoughts. Pinterest is used as a shape of on-line muse with the useful resource of artists, photographers, and certainly one of a type creative humans, and you can located it to apply as properly.

You might also additionally use it to increase the reach of your platform. On Pinterest, as a collector and curator of exciting matters, you can draw in people who percent your hobbies and are inquisitive about the matters that you and your business organization are interested in. It is possible to create an energetic, colorful community on Pinterest, whether or not or not or now not your cause is to sell books, promote education offerings, or pitch your e-book to a high publishing house. The sky's the restriction if you have a remarkable platform!

Pinterest advertising and marketing and advertising is a splendid opportunity for modern businesses because of all of the motives why. In this newsletter, we will cross over the primary steps of putting in place your on-line presence at the social media platform, starting with the manner to installation a successful employer Pinterest profile.

Creating a Vibrant Online Presence

Pinterest is easy and simple to apply, and it takes only a few minutes to get started out out. While you are having an tremendous time installing vicinity your Pinterest account with this notable new device, you may additionally take some measures to guarantee that you're laying a sturdy foundation for the future success of your company's Pinterest efforts.

By growing a robust foundation, I'll educate you a way to put the guidelines for a successful Pinterest advertising and marketing and advertising advertising and marketing and advertising and marketing advertising marketing campaign. I'll give an reason for how the registration method works, provide you with advice on the way to pick out out out which alternatives you can use to installation your account, and lead you via the system of making a compelling and informative profile to attract people in your internet page.

First and essential, you may want to request an account invitation from the internet internet page. Due to the reality that Pinterest is currently simplest available by way of invitation, you may each want to are searching for an invitation right now from Pinterest or ask an existing member to ask you. The reaction time from the internet net page varies; some folks that request invitations seem to get them proper away, whilst others seem to must wait longer—every now and then even weeks—for their invitations.

As a quit result, the simplest and only manner to get an invitation is to request one from a friend or coworker who has a Pinterest account. It's simple for a present day member to welcome their friends to the clubhouse. They only need to log into their Pinterest account, click on on on their profile call inside the top right corner, after which select the "Invite Friends" alternative from the drop-down menu that indicates at the proper. They can also additionally furthermore then select which Facebook buddies to invite, or they will be able to ship proper away electronic mail invites with the useful resource of selecting "Email" at the left-hand factor of the page, as seen in the screenshot underneath. You ought to get your invitation internal some days of that.

Once you've got been invited, you will see a big welcome show display that gives you with severa options for putting in vicinity your Pinterest account. Click at the link for your invitation email to go to the Pinterest sign-up web page.

Is it higher to hyperlink to Facebook or Twitter? What do you suspect?

When it involves connecting your Pinterest account to either your Facebook or your Twitter profile, you may find out your self having to make a choice even in advance than you get started out out. This is virtually so you can also employ Pinterest's social media sharing abilities, that would useful resource you within the development of your platform. Of path, this will increase the difficulty of which one to select out out.

Each has its private set of capacity benefits and drawbacks. When you sign up using Facebook, Pinterest will are attempting to find thru your buddies and automatically signal you up to examine any of your buddies who have already got a Pinterest account, until you specify in any other case. This may be a extraordinary way to get your Pinterest following off to a short start, as the various people you observe will reciprocate through following you again. However, if you do no longer use your private Facebook page for business company functions, or if you have other motives that make it not viable or mistaken in case you need to sign up for your individual profile in your Pinterest account, utilising Facebook to your organisation might not be an exquisite concept.

A Twitter account that you use for company business agency advertising can be associated on your Pinterest profile as properly, it is a smart possibility if your Twitter account is being used for business corporation advertising. For folks who simply have a non-public Twitter profile that they do no longer want related to their Pinterest account, they may constantly create a modern Twitter profile this is most effective for advertising and marketing and advertising and advertising and marketing and advertising reasons and positioned it to use for their Pinterest presence.

After you have assessed the advantages and disadvantages of each preference, pick out out the only that feels excellent for you and your corporation enterprise. If you aren't already logged into your Facebook or Twitter account, you may be required to achieve this before you could continue. Afterwards, you will be induced to furnish Pinterest permission to get entry to your Facebook or Twitter bills. You need to be aware that imparting Pinterest get admission to will no longer jeopardize the protection of your password or distinct statistics.

While growing your Pinterest account, if you choose out to perform that using Twitter, you'll be brought on to choose out a username. Because your username need to be fewer than 15 characters, you can want to hold it short and clean. Your username might be covered in the URL in your Pinterest profile, and other customers is probably able to view it as well. In order no longer to pick out a few detail that is too personal, humiliating, or may be compromising, you need to no longer pick out some issue that is too wide.

This is an amazing desire in case you recognize you will be the use of Pinterest best to promote your business enterprise and want to apply your commercial enterprise business enterprise name as your username. In addition, it is suitable to apply each your first and final names as your username. For instance, Nordstrom's department keep makes use of the Pinterest account "Nordstrom" to sell its merchandise.

Starting awesome Pinterest bills can be a exquisite possibility in case you want to use Pinterest as an person and as a organisation on the same time and are excessive approximately retaining the two worlds incredible. You may additionally benefit this via the use of growing separate debts, one collectively with your Facebook profile and the alternative collectively in conjunction with your Twitter account, respectively. However, I might pause and remember my alternatives earlier than intending. Having Pinterest money owed way installing double the art work and spending times the time on protection. Therefore, if it's miles feasible in case you want to just preserve one account, I might suggest you to perform that. Also, hold in thoughts that your enterprise organisation fans will like seeing some of your personal pins as it lets in them to get to recognize you better and accept as real with you more. As a end end result, in maximum conditions, there may be no need to hold your personal pins hidden out of your agency's lovers.

Aside from that, you can want to enter the e-mail cope with which you'd need for use for any destiny Pinterest contact. Keep in mind that, due to the person of Pinterest's operation, you can nearly actually get a huge amount of emails pertaining to Pinterest. So you likely want to get an electronic mail account as a way with a view to contend with a excessive stage of verbal exchange with out becoming bothersome. If having a committed Pinterest e-mail account on your company makes revel in for you and your agency, you may need to discover setting one up for it.

When you are completed, enter your password and click on on on "Create Account." After that, Pinterest will ask you to select out out a few issues that you are inquisitive about on the subsequent severa monitors. This simplest permits the internet website to generate some content material material material hints that will help you in getting commenced to your journey. After that, you may be requested to construct some preliminary boards. Pinboards (every so often called "boards") are collections of pins; we are going to bypass into greater element concerning pinboards in Chapter 3. Now that you've observe the whole lot, you need to experience loose to honestly receive Pinterest's default settings and to make your private pointers as well.

A few more administrative messages and hints might be shown for your display display in advance than you may be encouraged to click on on on the "Start Pinning!" button, on the manner to seem at the lowest of your display show screen. Your Pinterest account is now formally yours. You in the intervening time are able to begin enhancing it an awesome way to better represent your emblem and enterprise company dreams!

Creating a Vibrant Online Presence

When you region your cursor over your name inside the top proper corner of any web web page in the Pinterest interface, a dropdown menu will appear that incorporates all your account settings and picks. Select "Settings" from the drop-down menu to get right of access to and alternate your Pinterest profile

Preparing your Pinterest profile ought to be achieved with care; this is the first have an effect on you will make on particular Pinterest clients, some of whom have the capability to emerge as lovers and fanatics of your work or commercial enterprise business enterprise. Take it slow while developing your Pinterest profile considering it's going to act as a essential connection to your net internet site, Facebook web page, and Twitter presence, so positioned in the attempt now!

Name of the Profile

Business owners are faced with a difficult choice in relation to the first actual box on their profile page: do you need to connect on Pinterest the use of your private name or your organization name?

In the pinnacle right-hand corner of the Pinterest interface, click on your username, and then on Edit Profile Settings.

Settings.

Using your agency's name to promote your logo to the Pinterest network can be a completely effective method to gain out to your goal marketplace. In accordance with the way Pinterest operates, the names you post in those regions may be repeated to extraordinary Pinterest clients in hundreds of methods, which include emails and different places inside the platform's interface, as described above. As a end result, it is crucial which you carefully evaluate what you positioned into these areas.

Make certain that the terms are legible and diagnosed, no matter the choice you select. This isn't the region to be clever or to use a name like "WriTeRhgftdgrl*222" because it's going to maximum possibly certainly cause confusion a number of the readers! Keep it smooth via using the usage of honestly alphabetical letters (no longer numerals) and making your name clean to bear in mind. Please do not use this name in case you do no longer need an electronic mail notification with this call sent out in your enthusiasts.

It is important to enter a few issue inside the "Last Name" field on Pinterest, so in case you'd want to utilize your enterprise name however your emblem is crafted from a couple of word, you can without problems cut up the call into containers. Joe's Shoe Repair, for instance, may moreover furthermore located "Joe's" within the "First Name" form and "Shoe Repair" within the "Last Name" location as a way to pick out out themselves. Additionally, you could use a superstar within the Last Name Field to function an additional person whilst but meeting Pinterest's necessities for the closing name. However, you need to be conscious that the asterisk will seem on your profile in addition to in Pinterest's mechanically produced communications from you.

With the exception of your username (which we are going to cope with next), you aren't required to have a high-quality profile name on Pinterest. On Pinterest, as an example, there are numerous Beth Haydens to choose out from. You are loose to apply any profile call that makes feel for you and your organisation; however, you need to utilize every the number one and very last name sections to avoid confusion.

Username

When it consists of the Pinterest international, your username is a completely great area from your profile call. If you created your Pinterest account the use of Facebook, your username modified into generated for you; but, if you created your Pinterest account via Twitter, you have been delivered about to choose out a username for the duration of the registration machine.

Because your Pinterest profile URL will be depending on your username, it's far vital that you pick out some issue memorable. Therefore, which will set up a username that is exquisite from others, you could want to embody masses of for your username (for instance, "BethHayden23"). If the username you desire is already taken, Pinterest will let you know which you need choose an opportunity one.

Unless you're experiencing a essential hassle, I may want to advise that you refrain from seeking to regulate your username after you have have been given created your account. Otherwise, you run the risk of losing something lovers you can have formerly received. In distinctive terms, in case you are given the possibility to pick out your username, use warning!

About

Using the "About" vicinity, you can percentage a bit bit approximately yourself and the subjects which you want to region up about with the rest of the Pinterest community. You need to take benefit of this remarkable risk to reveal human beings in your emblem, consequently don't skip over out on this opportunity. Consider consist of facts together with:

What subjects you'll be pinning about may be determined out quickly.

Who it is that you are trying to touch (your best client). Your Pinterest goals (as an example, igniting a debate, teaching customers, amusing them, saving clients' time and power, and so forth).

This is the URL of your net web page. Although it will no longer be a live connection, it's miles a terrific concept but. Ought to consist of it at the notion of your "About" phase. (Alternatively, you can miss the "http://" and simply begin the URL with "www."

Location

In the event which you are a close-by company and could want exclusive Pinterest customers to apprehend in which are placed, you should in reality offer your vicinity on this phase. It is OK to go away the vicinity difficulty easy in case you are an internet-based absolutely completely organization and could pick out now not to (or do not want to) display your geographical information.

Website

This region allows you to go into the URL of your net net page. Because your Pinterest profile remarkable offers one place for selling a internet site, you ought to count on cautiously approximately what you need to install this section.

The majority of the time, you could need to provide a hyperlink to your primary internet site. However, there can be activities in which you could want to don't forget which incorporates a link to a incredible part of your net web site in your most critical net page. This may be a completely precise store that is without a doubt to be had to Pinterest clients, or it can be a touchdown web page that gives a unfastened document or specific giveaway to fanatics who be a part of up to your e-publication.

In our economic ruin on Pinterest method, we're going to pass into similarly element on identifying who you're trying to appeal to in your board, which might also additionally additionally have a power on some thing internet internet site you pick to appoint in this vicinity. For the time being, you may maintain to use your primary internet internet site. Changing the URL may be a easy method in the future if you make a decision to make a change.

Image for Your Profile

If you have a Twitter or Facebook account, Pinterest will automatically combine your profile photograph from the ones bills. If you will want to apply a notable image, you could upload one in the "Image" location of your profile net net page. The "Refresh from Facebook/Twitter" preference will allow Pinterest to appearance your social media profile for a state-of-the-art photo when you have a more contemporary image for your Facebook or Twitter profile that you'd need to embody for your pinboard.

In an try and boom emblem recognition, you could need to strive using your enterprise emblem as your Pinterest profile image. Yes, it is perfectly OK; just ensure that your brand includes the name of your company in a clean, easy-to-have a take a look at typeface simply so human beings recognize who you're and what your agency does. It would not damage to boom a square-long-established version of your logo for the reason of clarity, in order that it can resultseasily wholesome into the area furnished with the beneficial aid of Pinterest in your picture. Otherwise, your logo may be cropped in this form of manner that it isn't viable for your prospective lovers to examine it correctly.

Alternatives to Facebook

Regardless of whether or not or not you commenced your Pinterest account thru Facebook or Twitter, you have got the option to connect your Pinterest account to your non-public Facebook profile internet web page.

When I first commenced the use of Pinterest, I modified into frightened about doing so because of the truth I emerge as involved that each of my pins is probably posted one after the other on my Facebook timeline, and that my friends is probably buried under the large quantity of pictures and updates. But evidently I became right. Pinterest, alternatively, does this in a smooth and effective manner. Because the net page puts your pins collectively, they may be published on your Facebook timeline as a fixed in place of one after the alternative, so that you do now not have to worry about overloading your friends with too many pins.

Connecting your non-public Facebook page in conjunction with your Pinterest account is a wonderful opportunity if you are comfortable utilising your personal Facebook web page for enterprise reasons. In the occasion that you need to keep your private Facebook profile absolutely personal and you recognize that you may be making use of your Pinterest account to promote your business enterprise, it may be a smart concept to avoid linking the 2 money owed together. However, if you're ok with combining the two, feel free to connect them together!

According to the business enterprise, Pinterest does not will let you post your pins for your Facebook business internet internet page in a continuing way. However, it's far feasible that this functionality can be brought inside the future.

Embedding a Twitter hyperlink

You can also have the choice to "Link to Twitter" enabled while you create a cutting-edge-day account the usage of your Twitter profile because the idea for it. When your Pinterest profile is attached to your Twitter account on this manner, now not some factor is automatically posted on Pinterest. However, this connection does will will let you sync your profile pics and log in the use of your Twitter account if you so need.

Visibility

If you are using Pinterest for marketing talents, you will need to ensure that your profile may be visible in engines like google, so ensure that the "Hide Your Pinterest Profile from Search Engines" possibility is prepared to "Off."

What Comes Next?

As rapid as you've got finished making all of your Pinterest profile modifications, make sure to click on on on the massive "Save Profile" button placed at the lowest of your profile net web page.

If you want to make any modifications to your Pinterest profile settings, which consist of your profile picture, net web page URL, or social media possibilities, you can continuously click on to your profile name after which "Settings" to make the crucial adjustments.

Knowing a way to installation a a achievement Pinterest account and layout a captivating profile will help you increase your following and generate site visitors in your net website. You're prepared to begin the maximum a laugh part of the approach: pinning!

Your Plan of Action

The first step is to determine whether or no longer you need to link your Pinterest profile in your Facebook or Twitter account.

By filling within the About, Location, Website, and other relevant containers collectively together with your crucial employer records,

31

you'll be able to assemble a compelling profile that allows you to stand out from the group.

By clicking on your call (or company name) within the pinnacle-proper corner of your display, you may get proper of access in your profile and evaluation it with a vital eye. Is there some aspect you did not see? How likely is it that your first profile will make a great have an effect on on Pinterest customers?

Chapter 2: What Kind Of Person Do You Want To Attract?

Please endure with me at the same time as I speak a few factor that some people may additionally find scandalous. I admire your statistics. Is it viable if you need to sit down?

The massive marvel is that in case you do now not spend the time crucial to format your Pinterest advertising approach earlier than you start, your efforts are in all likelihood to be a total waste of time.

Defining your Pinterest method is the first step in identifying who you're seeking out to reap collectively with your advertising and marketing efforts on Pinterest and the manner you could flow about doing so. Before you start building your boards and pins, you need to finish this step. In addition, the more you look at those humans, the more probably it is that you'll be able to construct a real relationship with them. Defining your Pinterest approach may even resource you in maintaining your recognition on what is most crucial: generating leads and attracting customers at the social media platform. As a side gain, it'll also resource you in evaluating how Pinterest suits into your whole sales and advertising and marketing plan.

Throughout this bankruptcy, my purpose is to help you in defining your perfect purchaser and discussing how you can design your fabric on Pinterest in this form of manner that it is quite attractive to that first-class purchaser. Aside from that, I will remind you approximately the goal of social media promoting (which includes Pinterest advertising and advertising and advertising) in addition to the machine you want to keep away from being eliminated from the Pinterest birthday party due to your beside the point conduct.

The Process of Developing a Profile of Your Ideal Client

Does your ideal purchaser constitute a crystal-clean photo to your thoughts?

In my opinion, you currently have a few clients with whom you want taking detail, folks that thrill and invigorate you. Try to count on strolling with a consumer who's one or of your favorites and what it's far about working with them which you discover especially satisfying. In your opinion, what's it about helping this type of character this is so appealing?

David Meerman is the writer of this piece. David Scott changed into the primary man or woman to signify the idea of

A consumer character, as defined with the aid of creator Seth Godin in his ebook The New Rules of Marketing and Advertising, is a shape of consumer character.

The Best Ways to Reach Buyers Through the Use of Social Media, Online Video, Mobile Applications, Blogs, Press Releases, and Viral Marketing in a honest manner (that is the 1/3 version of the ebook). As Scott explains, growing a consumer man or woman (moreover called a extraordinary client) is one of the most essential duties your enterprise organization can do earlier than beginning social media campaigns and carrying out out to clients via on line systems, among various matters.

It's as clean as writing out a thorough description of the sort of client you're trying to trap to your client personality (furthermore referred to as a first-rate client). It is vital to to start with boom those varieties of profiles that permits you to effectively outline your net technique before shifting in addition.

In his e-book, The New Rules of Marketing and Public Relations, Scott describes the subsequent test, which have grow to be finished with the aid of way of a specific institution an terrific manner to installation their consumer personas:

By categorizing clients into separate businesses after which cataloguing the records we recognise approximately every company, we are able to make it an entire lot a whole lot less hard to generate content material this is perfect to each number one demographic company. Alumni pride with a university internet website on line, as an example, is important in persuading them to make ordinary financial contributions to the agency wherein they earned their education. Young alumni (folks that graduated in the previous 10 or 15 years) and elderly alumni are customer personas that a university may have, depending on the age of the students that attended the college. In addition to one in all a kind technique, college officers need to recruit college students with the resource of encouraging them to interact in the software program method. In order for a university internet website online to gain fulfillment, it want to feature a client personality for the immoderate faculty scholar who is considering attending college. However, due to the fact that ability students' mother and father have pretty amazing informational desires than potential university college students themselves, the net internet web page designers may additionally determine to construct a separate customer man or woman for mother and father. An extra want for a university is to maintain the happiness of its current-day clients (contemporary college students). According to these findings, an powerful university website should possibly aim five superb client personas... In order to generate relevant content, the university will want to have a whole knowledge of the dreams and approaches of thinking of the 5 purchaser personas beneath interest.

When it consists of developing extraordinary, useable purchaser character profiles, one of the most a success strategies is to connect to them without delay on the deliver, which entails interviewing them. Ask when you have direct get right of access to to some of your chosen clients and if you'll be able to chat with them for a couple of minutes over the smartphone when you have that desire to be had.

A smart approach to comply with is to ask as many questions as you probable can in an effort to understand as hundreds as you probable can approximately each corporation of humans you stumble upon. What are their some time, exactly? Do they have a circle of relatives of their very personal or do they live with someone else? When humans first wake up within the morning, what specific subjects are on their minds? What terms and phrases do they use to give an explanation for themselves and the difficulties they may be coping with?

What do they love to do of their unfastened time to pass the time? Is there a internet site or social media platform that they make use of that I ought to recognize approximately? Exactly what makes people satisfied is a mystery to me.

The facts you got might be used to construct large profiles of every shape of patron you are trying to get into your agency. Take notice of the profile's description and image, and then put up it in a top notch place to your administrative center to serve as a reminder to all people in your organization. You may also additionally deliver each profile a nickname to help you preserve in mind their choices or distinguishing trends, on the aspect of "Sally the Bride-to-Be" or "John the Coach," to make it less difficult to take into account them.

Oreck (@oreck), a manufacturer of vacuum cleaners, air purifiers, and awesome small tool, markets its products on the whole to ladies as its perfect customers. Oreck marketers may need to likely convey collectively an entire high-quality-customer profile named "Suzy

39

Homemaker" and fill it with statistics about Suzy's dwelling scenario, whether or not or not she has kids or pets, and her pursuits. The United States Army (@usarmy) may additionally have an entire lot of 1-of-a-kind profiles, which encompass the ones of younger males and females who need to sign up within the military and individuals of the overall public who need to expose their guide for our squaddies.

Although this interest might also appear small to you, do no longer disregard its significance. The extra about the customers you are attempting to purpose on Pinterest, the greater effective you'll be at interacting with them via your advertising and marketing and advertising efforts. Learn extra about Pinterest right proper right here.

What Do You Want Your Ideal Client to Have?

Following your definition of your perfect customer and your research into analyzing all you can about him or her, you'll be in a miles higher characteristic to begin installing your Pinterest account.

Keeping your eye in your best client even as you are pinning will will can help you create pins and forums which can be some distance extra attractive on your target market. Take into interest the numerous patron personas at the same time as deciding on whether or not or no longer or now not to pin a image or video on your board. Would this be useful, instructive, thrilling, or inspirational to my outstanding client?" is a query you want to ask your self earlier than publishing a few issue. If you replied certain, then begin pinning! If it does no longer, begin attempting to find some aspect that does fall into this type of training.

With their Pinterest boards, the enterprise company Pretzel Crisps (@PretzelCrips) does an incredible procedure of speaking with its goal customers and opportunities. Besides the usage of their pins to provide extremely good thoughts for a way to make use of their merchandise (appetizers, dips, and so forth), this savvy snack corporation has stuffed their forums with extra snap shots and thoughts that its fans and fans like. They actually have a board titled "Genius," that is entire of contemporary and revolutionary mind for every the residence and the workplace. Pretzel Crisps' cloth is appealing to the people they're trying to goal because the employer business enterprise is acquainted with precisely who they will be trying to gain.

The AARP (@AARP Official) is truely every other example of a employer that has finished an powerful Pinterest technique. The Pinterest account of this club company is only a few months vintage, however they have already made an affect: they have got created forums with catchy names that appeal to their intention demographic of the aged, in conjunction with "501 Technology" and "Movies for Grownups." Senior users on Pinterest are well conscious that this cloth is customized absolutely to their desires and hobbies, as established through the use of the usage of the fact that it is been customized mainly for the 501 goal marketplace. And whilst purchasers see that you've placed inside the try to find out precisely what they need, they'll be more likely to move back.

Pinterest Can Be a Part of Your Overall Marketing Strategy If You Use It Right

In the maelstrom this is social media, it is easy to get bewildered. We may also delude ourselves into believing that we're being certainly effective by means of manner of spending 10 hours a day speakme with human beings on some of systems thru using social media web sites along with Facebook, Twitter, LinkedIn, Google 1, and Pinterest. Aside from that, it seems as even though a present day social media tool is created each six months, with social media experts yelling which you need to have a presence on the most recent internet site, in any other case your business can be doomed from the start.

Simply lighten up, take a deep breath, and allow the circus song wash over you in the historical past. Let me dispel some not unusual misconceptions that have persisted at some degree within the years.

When it entails on line advertising and marketing and advertising and marketing, your desires are easy: you need to increase profits. Promote your net web website via the use of riding traffic once more to it, obtaining new individuals in your mailing list, and changing website traffic into paying clients.

Consider your marketing technique to be just like a bicycle wheel, with the spokes representing your intention demographic and the hub representing your business business corporation. Your content material-wealthy internet site or blog serves as the hub of this wheel, with social networking net web sites collectively with Facebook, Twitter, and Pinterest serving because the spokes. And, but the reality that they're very critical spokes, they're nonetheless genuinely that: spokes. According to specialists, distribution and location web site visitors generation on your net web page's exceptional content cloth should be finished through the usage of social media systems. It moreover can't be emphasised how vital it's far to installation relationships and trust on social media systems. Alternatively, if the humans with whom you're developing those connections by no means depart your Pinterest profile or Facebook page, you are losing it sluggish (and probable dropping a number of time).

As with each exceptional social networking net web web page, Pinterest functions within the identical manner. It may be important to reconsider your Pinterest approach in case your efforts are not most important to an boom in clients coming thru your door.

Period.

We should continuously take into account that taking element in social media circles is a technique to an prevent, now not an end in and of itself. We have to address it as such.

To start, growth a listing of your desires and goals earlier than intending any farther with this technique. In order to assure that your Pinterest efforts aren't in useless, you may want to preserve in mind setting the ones desires wherever you may see them on a commonplace basis (for instance, above your computer show or over your laptop). Establishing relationships is crucial, however you need to do it in a manner so you can useful resource you in project your large goals.

Allow your individuality to shine through

Before you begin pinning—in truth, earlier than you even set up your account—you and your institution want to pick out topics which you are obsessed on and that would function springboards for developing splendid content fabric on Pinterest. Pinterest's logo call includes the time period "interest," so do not dedicate the cardinal sin of being dull with the aid of manner of pinning some aspect that is not interesting.

On her Pinterest internet web web page, she lets in the spirit of her company to show via. One board, "The Wander Wall," consists of photographs, advice, tips, and private testimonies curated via numerous of the arena's superb-entire-time tour bloggers. She additionally has other boards which can be traditional of what you would count on from a tour blogger, along with one referred to as "The Wander Wall," which includes pix, recommendation, pointers, and private reminiscences from numerous of the area's quality full-time tour bloggers. Salvon moreover has boards dedicated to greater unusual topics, which embody her "VW and Tiny Dwellings" board, which is devoted to minimalist dwelling areas together with Volkswagen buses and itty-bitty houses, among different subjects. It's a cute, one-of-a-type board this is virtually steady with the logo, however it's also exquisite and sticky. This particular fabric might be remembered in a while, passed on thru social media, and could allow humans to engage with Salvon because of its a laugh nature.

Additionally, preserve in thoughts that at the identical time as determining a way to attain your goal purchaser the usage of Pinterest, you could employ pix and movies to speak the concept in the again of your business enterprise. What do you want your organization to be diagnosed for? What are the agency's middle beliefs and requirements? What type of way of lifestyles is it seeking to sell and why does that lifestyle appeal for your purpose client? Those are the questions you need to answer.

Consider BlogFrog, a platform that lets in writers gain traffic and construct corporations. The agency's cute logo, the frog, is prominently displayed at the business enterprise's Pinterest web page in an tremendous Pinterest method. The BlogFrog institution pins pictures and films which may be associated with their target demographic of woman bloggers so that you can acquire them. Their BlogFrog Fashion board is even saved up to date with the beneficial useful resource of them. More than most effective a everyday style board, notwithstanding the reality that, this one includes clothes and accessories in BlogFrog's signature pink colour, in addition to distinctive items from the agency's collections (green, of route). In spite of the pictures being humorous and amusingly cute, BlogFrog manages to walk an fantastic line amongst below-promoting (via no longer citing the brand or its merchandise at all) and over-promoting (via forcing the logo down humans's throats at each opportunity)... In phrases of Pinterest advertising, BlogFrog's advertisements strike the right stability among originality and application.

If you pin things that you are enthusiastic about and that display off your man or woman, your enthusiasm can be contagious, and you could create engaging content material cloth that your fanatics will like, similarly to a following of your personal on social media structures.

Chapter 3: Become A Valuable Source Of Knowledge

The Pinterest board pinners for Chobani yogurt are probably the greatest within the industry. If a employer desires to get the most out of Pinterest, it has to do extra than genuinely upload photographs from its very own website. Since they apprehend what their customers want, they instead create instructive forums and pins.

Multiple Chobani (@chobani) forums offer recipes from many internet websites and blogs. Many of the recipes use yogurt, despite the fact that not they all do. Yogurt producers comprehend well that almost all of grocery purchasing is finished through manner of girls, and that they may be constantly searching out glowing and clean recipes to feed their developing families with. Chobani's pinners aren't definitely spreading hyperlinks to their website; they'll be inside the commercial enterprise organization of assisting their lovers. A secondary gain of Chobani's recipe pins is that they educate clients approximately its yogurt, notwithstanding the fact that that is not the precept reason.

The Chobani net internet site online gives records and sources with out imposing any form of economic or distinct obligation on its website on line site visitors.

People aren't interested by what you have to provide due to its private traits. Your products and services are in excessive name for due to the reality they may assist customers in resolving their problems. In the eyes of capability clients, Pinterest is a dependable deliver of statistics. Instead of seeing yourself as a salesclerk, you'll be visible as a useful resource for expertise and concept, so that you can assist you be greater a fulfillment on Pinterest.

Ann Handley and C.C. Chapman, the authors of the Content Rules, urge you to be a source of facts on line:

A accurate piece of content material fabric does no longer promote itself; as an alternative, it explains or solves a hassle. In different terms, it'd not assist you are making coins by using selling your gadgets or conveying messages which may be imagined to perform that. To the other, it establishes your enterprise agency's credibility as a reliable and massive supply for provider-independent facts...

Posting captivating material on social networking net web sites like Pinterest and others is a first-rate concept. Self-selling and self-indulgence, but, are

The greater you operate Pinterest's capabilities to hold your brand's personality and pin in your goal marketplace, the greater equipped you may be to apprehend precisely what to place up and the way to do it. It's a outstanding area to place those talents to the take a look at. In order to get the most from your Pinterest advertising approach, you will need to mix it with the relaxation of your internet marketing method.

It's time to get all of the manner all the manner all the way down to business employer and discover ways to pin now which you've described your Pinterest marketing desires and approach.

Boards which can be visually appealing, similarly to driving pins

When it entails its assignment statement on its internet website, Pinterest states that its purpose is "to bring humans together with the aid of sharing the subjects they discover interesting." People who percent an hobby in a e-book, toy, or delicacies also can have a mutual link, we expect. People from the world over are meeting on Pinterest due to the large style of pins which may be being shared every week. In order to connect people, Pinterest uses pins and pinboards as of its maximum big capabilities.

It's feasible to your organisation to apply pins to construct connections, create a experience of community, and trap the right kinds of customers. Because of Pinterest's primary patron interface, this is a surely easy device to perform.

To set up your images on Pinterest, you may create a "pinboard" (a grouping of pins) and categorize them in numerous techniques. In this financial disaster, we're going to undergo the many strategies for pinning images on social media and a few suggestions for developing thrilling content material which will draw a massive target market.

Boards

Pinboards (from time to time called "forums") are virtual bulletin boards in which Pinterest customers can also furthermore gather and set up pix that they discover thrilling or interesting. "Blogging and social media suggestions," "Pinterest is wonderful for commercial enterprise employer," "Writers and writing," "Killer advertising and marketing advice," and "Killer marketing recommendation," to call some of my many boards.This board additionally includes 'Killer Marketing Advice,' "I Believe," and "Amusing," among exclusive subjects.This is in which most of the pins I gather on a every day basis come to be. Furthermore, I've have been given forums committed to the whole thing from specific to redecorating to realistic suggestions for planning future journeys.

The vacuum purifier producer, Oreck (@oreck), has a Pinterest web web page titled "Clean Made Easy" that gives recommendation on the way to efficiently easy your home, inclusive of a way to easy your glass variety, residing room baseboards, and gold rings. In keeping with the internet site's tagline

"Clean Made Easy" is the call of Oreck's internet site, so the call of the board is quite apt from a branding thing of view.

Board names are an essential part of any undertaking.

Creating a very specific name for each board you construct is an important part of the approach. Newbies to the web net web page will in all likelihood begin with the beneficial resource of growing a big variety of "big" forums that allow them to pin numerous pics at the equal subject matter. Then once more, I'd need to hassle a caution examine: do not do it.

Yes, it appears to be a clean manner to collect a huge range of severa photos in a unmarried spot. In evaluation, you want to be as specific as possible at the facet of your board subjects and titles. This board ought to now not be called "cruises," however as an opportunity "Fun Family Caribbean Cruises," that could be a ways greater specific and memorable to passengers. However, many commercial business enterprise proprietors are aware of the importance of the distinction. When it includes the goods and services they use, customers have a large kind of alternatives. Which of those boards may also you recommend to a pal who's thinking about taking her family on a Caribbean cruise to Aruba?

It's moreover a brilliant concept to hold your board names succinct, snappy, and to the issue. As a forestall give up end result, if you need to get a person to conform with you on Pinterest, you need to make certain that your board names are attractive and appealing to the individual that sees them.

Visitors to a member's profile page will now see a thumbnail instance in their forums in the most current version of their Pinterest profile (as of March 2012). There is an trouble with this new factor of view given that lengthy board names can be reduce off on this profile web web page, that is unwanted. As a end result, the significance of smart names can be obscured via translation. Aside from the truth that the name of your board may be reduce off in your profile internet net page, there can be some different motive to hold your board names to no greater than 5 or six phrases in duration.

The Travel Channel (@travelchannel) has honed the paintings of making brief, compelling board names with the aid of way of manner of the use of titles like "Travel Bucket List" and "Festivals & Events," amongst others. Travel writer Jodi Ettenberg (@jodiettenberg) has a slew of catchy Pinterest board titles, like "timber that appear to be broccoli" (see Figure four.1). Has that call ever stuck your hobby and made you want to test out her board a hint extra intently?

An individual URL may be assigned to a fantastic pinboard. I'll use my non-public famous board, "Pinterest is Great for Your Biz," as an example: http://www.Pinterest.Com/bethhayden/pinterest is Beneficial to Your Business

If you would love, you could embed this board into your net site, electronic mail it to a friend, or proportion it for your social media payments on Facebook or Twitter. If you replica and paste the decision of the board into the url bar, you may speedy get to this collection of pins.

If you eventually exchange the decision of your board, Pinterest may even alternate the URL of the board you set up. This is a cautionary tale. It might not don't forget which social media platform you operate to hook up with the board: Facebook, Twitter, or your personal personal or business organisation website on-line.

Jodi Ettenberg (@jodiettenberg) is a board name fashion designer who likes to make names which may be short, specific, and splendid.

If the hyperlink is in your corporation's net web site or any other internet website on line, you can want to update it straight away.

On the difficulty of forums, one in addition difficulty to mention: each board on Pinterest may additionally moreover have a cover photo which you edit, and this photograph may be visible out of your profile internet page and one-of-a-type regions of the web web page. By clicking at the name of your Pinterest account in the higher proper corner of your display display screen whilst you are on the Pinterest domestic web page, you may be taken proper away for your profile internet web page on the internet site on-line. Following that, whilst you hover over any of the boards to your profile, you could see a field that reads "Edit Board Cover." Click on that container to edit the board cowl. To make adjustments to the board cover, click on on on at the picture. As rapid as you select out that desire, Pinterest will set off you to pick out a image for use as the duvet photo for the corresponding board at the web web page. Remember to choose out snap shots which may be clean and smooth to recognize for the covers of your boards as a manner to get human beings to go to those forums!

How to Make Use of a Pin

As we've were given formerly stated, Pinterest permits clients to create subject-based absolutely sincerely photograph organizations, which is probably referred to as "boards," on the internet web web page. A pin, rather than a unmarried photograph for your collections, is used to consult every of the photos to your collections. A pin, in location of a unmarried picture to your collections, is really a bit of cloth that you have published to taken into consideration certainly one of your forums. When possible, every pin has a link to a distinctive net web site that has extra information about the picture.

To pin a picture to one in all your boards, you have got got three alternatives: 1) Move the photograph to the board.2) Move the picture to some different board.

1. Save a picture on your internet browser thru the use of the Pin It bookmarklet.

The 2d technique is to copy and paste a hyperlink to a image into your net browser.

Upload a image of your very non-public to the gallery.

Each of them may be tested in further element under.

The first technique is to make use of the Pin It bookmarklet on your browser.

Using the Pin It bookmarklet, which provides a "Pin It" button on your browser's toolbar, is with the resource of way of a ways the fastest and best way to pin a photo.

If you have not already, create an account on Pinterest and download the Pin It bookmarklet (which may be placed at www.Pinterest.Com/about/candies) if you haven't already.

When you operate the bookmarklet, you may immediately save an image from any internet internet web page for your Pinterest board without leaving your browser. The Pin It bookmarklet button may be placed for your browser's toolbar in case you're presently on a web internet page or weblog placed up and need to keep an photo from that internet web page or weblog put up. Once you've got were given finished that, Pinterest will open a pop-up window wherein you may pick out out the photo or video you want to pin from that net website, and it'll ask you what board and outline you need to apply in your pin within the approach. A description of each pin have to be included with every pin. As speedy as the pin is positioned to your board via Pinterest, it'll routinely get its URL. When the pin is put on your board, Pinterest will routinely get its URL.

The following is a excellent time-saving inspiration: Additionally, the bookmarklet might also robotically fill within the description of a pin for you even as you click on it. Use your bookmark bar to select out any text from the net web page you preference to save (such as the blog submit identify or a in particular tasty paragraph from an editorial) earlier than hitting the "Pin It" button to save it for your pc. Then, to maintain the photograph, click on at the "Pin It" icon to the proper of the photograph. The description of the pin might be generated mechanically from the wording you've got selected for it. While pinning short and now not looking to spend time being current together together with your descriptions, this approach may additionally prevent a massive quantity of effort and time.

Additionally, the pins need to still be related to the picture's specific supply, and so forth. In Chapter fourteen, you may be aware additional records concerning ethical promise, which you want to browse.

Repinning

It is moreover ability to repin remarkable human beings's pins on Pinterest, during a comparable thanks to but you could retweet a few factor on the Twitter social media internet internet site on-line. Normally, you may now not repin any individual else's pin until you definitely likeable the photo on it pin and had to place it on one amongst your very personal forums; in any other case, you'll no longer repin.

Headlines and outlines that square degree compelling square degree enclosed.

For each ikon you pin, you'll be needed to deliver a short description of what you are promise to the board. Do not neglect giving cautious interest to the current thinking about the truth that a charming description has the potential to create a massive difference in whether or not or not or not your ikon is shared the diverse individuals of Pinterest's network. Writing super captions on your images is vital if you choice them to be shared and, as a quit result, growth the amount of human beings United Nations corporation business enterprise have a look at you on social media.

Your pin's description place may encompass as a lot as five hundred characters, constant with Pinterest's guidelines. If one line or one phrase is all it is required to as it should be describe your photo, your description may also be as quick collectively line or one phrase; in spite of the truth that, it must be important to create it severa pages long in distinct times. A favored rule of thumb is to apply the ideal phrases that you just want to talk in order to be as curt as capacity. The naked minimum of characters is needed to very well give an explanation for your image and offer context in your fanatics— and no longer a unmarried in addition character. To write masses of terms isn't an wonderful concept, however if many pages are needed to definitely describe an photo, pass ahead and write pretty a few phrases.

Here are a few examples of proper descriptions:

Keep your virtual digicam lenses in tip-top shape with this cleaning advice, "reads the caption of a photograph of a slew of cameras that consequences in a snap shots internet internet site."

Here's a hyperlink to an academic Flickr put up about "I've been seeking out a few element much like this to reveal my clients." The guide's identify is "A Complete Guide to Finding and Using Incredible Flickr Images." Bloggers searching out pics to make use of of their blog posts can also moreover discover this material sincerely useful. "

These descriptions are undeniably more captivating and instructive than terms like "Wow" or "This is terrific."

Check that your description fits the content cloth cloth of the pin similarly to the URL that it refers customers to. Keep your bait-and-switch strategies hidden and avoid duping people into clicking to your pin under faux pretenses. In business company, whether or not or not or now not on Pinterest or in each exclusive profession, honesty is typically the superb coverage.

While writing your descriptions, I extraordinarily advocate you add a few man or woman for your writing. As a very last results, I've located that many pinners do not take the time to surely fill out their descriptions, ensuing in descriptions which can be without a doubt stupid. You want to inform a story, which encompass a letter expressing why you're happy with the pin, otherwise you need to infuse some persona into the outline of the pin. Figure 4.Three shows my splendid-performing pin, as well as a brief description of what it accomplishes.

Also, do no longer be afraid to provide a few private records approximately yourself. For instance, suppose you have got were given a hidden longing for a few element, a thriller responsible satisfaction, in any other case you aren't as organized as you'll need to be. Current and capacity clients will admire your being trustworthy, and they may almost simply sense that they've some element in common with you! You have to moreover be able to explicit yourself as a very specific person. While your personnel may be posting as a fixed on Pinterest, it's miles important to let them realize that they will be themselves on the social media community. Finally, we need to do business enterprise with a person we like, and it's far hundreds less complicated to like someone while they're allowed to let their hair down a bit.

Getting your functionality clients to understand, like, and do not forget you is the appropriate trinity for social media relationships. You've set up a excellent foundation in your clients to become definitely unswerving if you can supply them the opportunity to get to recognize you, like you, and in the end remember you thru your content and dating-constructing sports activities. When you pin some issue, it gives you records.

Chapter 4: Getting In Touch With Pinterest Users

Now that you've finished the setup of your Pinterest profile and feature started out pinning snap shots and arranging your forums, you will want to begin setting up a following among your enthusiasts. People who observe your Pinterest profile or your precise boards are known as (because it should be) fans inside the global of Pinterest.

Your Pinterest enthusiasts are without a doubt as good sized as your Facebook friends and fans, in addition for your Twitter followers. And one of the exceptional techniques to get them is to make the maximum of the covered connections on Pinterest.

In Chapter eight, we're going to pass into similarly intensity on the way to enlarge and maintain relationships along side your lovers. For the time being, allow's test the four number one methods in which Pinterest clients communicate with one another.

Commenting

When you comment on Pinterest, it sincerely works exactly the identical way as when you touch upon Facebook. It is viable to leave a brief reaction beneath any man or woman's pin (or one in every of your own). Simply located your reaction inside the area below the pin that says "Add a statement," then click on on the "Post Reply" button to put up it.

When you statement, ensure you are contributing some thing worthwhile to the subject due to the fact a pin is the start of a communicate! (See Figure 5.1 for an example.) Make certain you're bringing some element exciting or beneficial to the subject, irrespective of whether or now not you are the first or the seventy-first man or woman to observation. Consider supplying an example by using way of agreeing with the alternative person's function, disagreeing courteously, or explaining why you revel in the character's pin or board.

During your comments, it's far useful to consider your self as someone who is attending a cocktail celebration, that is an exquisite assessment to keep in thoughts. In the same way, you would not interrupt a group of people speakme in an effort to make an aggressive income pitch; in the equal manner, you should not interrupt a speak on Pinterest in order to marketplace your gadgets and services.

offerings. Unlike unique social media systems, Pinterest discourages over-promotion, as it does in almost all forms of advertising and marketing and advertising in recent times— which include conventional print media.

Tagging

Using the hashtag # Pinteresttag will permit you to mention unique Pinterest customers to your remarks or sell a particular pin to them, that allows you to allow them to look it.

The maximum green way to accumulate this is to begin coming into the choice of the individual you need to tag right now after typing the @ image. Following that, Pinterest will provide you with a drop-down menu of customers from whom you can pick.

Using tagging, you could with out problem make hints to your modern-day and capability customers approximately subjects and pins that you're feeling they could like. If you need, you could moreover engage with them by way of asking them questions, mastering approximately their research together together with your merchandise, or absolutely learning more about them and the shape of Pinterest content material cloth that they find out charming and useful. Recall that the cause is to bring together relationships with human beings, so pick your tags cautiously. Don't be a deliver of infection to clearly anybody!

A be aware is probably despatched to your e mail address at the equal time as a person mentions you in a Pinterest comment. In this situation, the person who wrote the remark is attempting to find to attract you into the talk in some way, and a few humans view this as an possibility to installation a private reference to the person who submitted the observation. For those who have already been tagged, make certain to appearance whether the individual that tagged you has any questions or feedback, after which react to them!

Liking

Status updates, feedback, and photos are comparable to Facebook's reputation updates, comments, and pictures in that you could "As" a pin through clicking on its image, much like you could do with a standing replace, declaration, or photo on Facebook. To deliver your approval of a person's art work in a brief and easy way, use this technique. When you "like" a pin, you are not sharing it together along with your lovers within the same manner that you can at the same time as you "repin" some thing; as an alternative, you are simply giving the pin a chunk nod of approval by clicking the "Like" button on the pin. In order to "like" a pin for your Pinterest home web page, you want to first hover your mouse over the pin till a "like" button seems on your screen. All you need to do now could be click on on the button to expose your consent.

Likes are absolutely optional, however they're a first rate manner to have interaction with special human beings and create relationships at the social media platform. The huge shape of likes you have received is likewise saved on file through Pinterest, which can be visible thru heading in your Pinterest domestic web page and deciding on "Likes" (this is located beneath your profile name). It is feasible to move lower lower back and be aware pins that you have favored in a previous session by way of the usage of using this capability. In the event that you choice to touch upon or embed a pin you have got desired later in a weblog publish, having this statistics reachable may be beneficial. In-depth facts on a manner to contain Pinterest pins into your weblog posts may be explored in more detail

"56 Ways to Promote Your Business on Pinterest," which I wrote as a traveler publish for Copyblogger in February 2012, come to be a large hit and acquired loads of pinning (pins).It grow to be my intention to like as lots of the ones pins as I possibly ought to, and then I published a comment on each one to convey my appreciation to the pinner for his or her time and paintings. It become thru this technique that I changed into able to get a great range of new followers, similarly to find a few exceptional new pinners to observe!

Hashtags

Hashtags are used to categorize remarks and descriptions on Pinterest, and they may be considerably applied to categorize communications in brand new. For example, as seen in Figure five.2, you may clearly use the # image without delay earlier than key phrases or troubles to your remarks, with out setting a region the various # image and both the phrase itself or many of the terms themselves. By tagging your pins and forums, you are making it a great deal much less complex for others to discover and use your artwork. Hashtags on Pinterest, together with those for "infographics," "weddings," and "recipes," are a number of the maximum famous at the net web site. You can also use hashtags which you format yourself or ones that you find out on Pinterest to market it your business organization organisation's products and services.

With using hashtags, users might also moreover redecorate the # sign and any terms that appear after it right right right into a hyperlink that they could use to discover specific pins which may be comparable in problem depend range. By clicking at the hashtag #recipes, for example, customers will be despatched to an internet web web page providing the most cutting-edge recipes from the popular recipe sharing internet website online Pinterest (with the most present day ones on the top of the page).

When Pinterest grows in popularity, I trust that the organisation will boom its usage of hashtags and decorate the functioning of its searching for device. To start with, you may use hashtags to highlight the principle concept of your pin similarly to to find out different pins which might be connected on your non-public.

Establishing a Personal Relationship with Your Ideal Customer

The development of an top notch purchaser profile, which may be carried out to resource inside the development of your Pinterest approach, become defined in Chapter 3. If you need to make the most of Pinterest's connection capacity, it's far important to consider that your ideal consumer is someone who makes use of social media because of the truth he or she likes being sociable on a huge level.

What you want to do is locate feedback, tagging, likes, and hashtags in the spirit of forging a dating with the individual with whom you're speaking. When team of workers interact in actual, heat, one-on-one connection with customers and clients, no longer something makes a business corporation seem greater human — and consequently more tempting — than witnessing them reap this (whether or no longer in character or on social media). In truth, this is precisely what those techniques offer you the functionality to do!

The Influence of Photographs

There is a trouble with Tamara Suttle, LPC (@tamaragsuttle), an authorized expert counselor who uses Twitter. She works with new therapists, lots of whom are truely untrained, and he or she or he preferred to reveal them a way to create a pleasing and alluring therapist's place of job environment for their clients. A video come to be produced to show her approach. In fact, lots of those therapists are simply getting began out in their careers and feature in no way had to set up a therapist's workplace in advance than—in fact, numerous of them have in no way even stepped foot in one in advance than.

As Suttle mentioned to them, "you want to reflect onconsideration on the impact your administrative center has to your consumers' perception of you." It's "crucial to create a first rate first impact," says the writer. Nonetheless, regardless of the fact that the phrases "heat" and "inviting" are easy to say, putting them into motion with regards to developing an environment in a actual-global place of business is substantially more tough to do. Even springing up with the terms to provide an purpose behind what a "welcoming place of work" looks as if is a hard mission. In flip, whilst Suttle began out using Pinterest, she observed that it had substantial ability.

Her "Private Practice from the Inside Out" board, which she titled "Private Practice from the Inside Out," speedy grew right into a amazing series of thoughts and suggestions regarding the topic, beginning with assets about waiting rooms and office regions and fast increasing. Real-lifestyles pics of treatment workplaces, in addition to recipes she's published (manner to movie big call chef Jamie Oliver), are only some times of what she's positioned on her Pinterest web page. Those reading remedy or strolling within the vicinity who are attempting to find hints on how to installation their very first healing room will find out a plethora of alternatives proper right here. The electricity of pix makes Suttle's expert recommendation clean and easy to apprehend in this video. She does a high-quality interest.

Oreck (@oreck) got here up with a way to use seen material on Pinterest that works thoroughly.

Our method to content cloth is straightforward: we pin stuff that we feel our clients could locate thrilling to our Pinterest board. We spend a extensive quantity of time at the telephone.

It is possible to attach this to Oreck, our products, or our guiding values in a few manner. Despite the truth that we've got were given have been given a board for each of our most recent objects (along side vacuums, air purifiers, and steam mops), it best capabilities snap shots of the topics in actual humans's houses, plenty of which come from the bloggers with whom we cooperate as a part of our blogger outreach marketing campaign.

The truth is that we do no longer need to be like such plenty of notable organizations who've all of their product photos posted on their net web sites. Our boards encompass education collectively with "Furry Friends" [which includes images of beautiful puppies] and "Magnificent Floors" [which contains photographs of stunning home flooring choices] to assist us gain this goal. In truth, our [our "signature"] blue coloration is the scenario of a board this is absolutely dedicated to it... Simply due to the reality it's far visually appealing.

We want to increase a relationship collectively together together with her via her dogs, her particular floor surfaces, or a favourite coloration that lets in you to remind her of the answers Oreck products can also provide to satisfy the dreams in her home and make her lifestyles a piece bit less difficult.

When it involves accomplishing their goals, Tamara Suttle and Oreck have mastered the artwork of harnessing the energy of pictures. You can discover both of them on Pinterest, growing unique and attractive content material cloth for their followers. They have every agreed to take at the position of content material material material manufacturers for his or her followers at the social media community.

Things to Keep in Mind When Publishing Content on Pinterest

When you rent social media sites along with Facebook, Twitter, and Pinterest, you should take on the characteristic of a content material marketer to be able to collect achievement. In the phrases of Social Media Examiner, this is one of the maximum well-known and well-known social media blogs on the net, this option is as follows:

Content advertising and marketing is the approach of making and freely sharing informative content material with the aim of converting prospects into clients and customers into repeat clients. Repeated and everyday publicity [to content] builds a relevant dating that offers a couple of possibilities for conversion, in preference to a "one-shot" all-or-no longer something income technique.

A realistic marketer distributes fabric via numerous channels, along with his or her internet site, Twitter feed, and YouTube channel. Your platform on Pinterest is absolutely a few extraordinary extension of that content material material marketing method; the handiest difference is that every one of the material is seen in place of textual in nature (i.E., pix and movies). The center standards of content fabric material advertising and marketing and advertising and advertising are precisely similar to they're for a few different form of advertising.

To correctly sell on social media systems, you want to ensure that each piece of content you upload both solves an trouble to your aim customers or entertains them—ideally each—and that it does so normally. This "Share or Solve; Don't Shill" philosophy, as articulated with the resource of Content Rules authors Ann Handley and C.C. Chapman, is important to the achievement of net advertising and marketing. Once you have established a incredible reference to your audience through the excellent content material material you produce on your internet website (and exceptional social media structures), they will be much more likely to shop for from you given that they receive as genuine with and prefer you. When you skip the very vital step of making quality content fabric and alternatively deliver out fluff or income messages, your target marketplace will lose religion in you, and your online web site visitors and social media interactions will in no manner alternate into customers or customers.

Something that can be useful while thinking about whether or not or no longer or not or no longer to place up a piece of fabric on Pinterest is to evaluate the way you need humans to experience after seeing a certain photo or video. The reality that seen information can be honestly charming and emotive approach that you may truly elicit unique sentiments for your aim market—preferably precise ones which includes satisfaction, pride, contentment, or interest—via supplying them with appealing visual cloth. So first remember the manner you need your target audience to revel in, after which hold in mind if your photograph or video adds to that sensation or now not. If it virtually works, congratulations; you have got got a winner on your arms! If this is the case, located the mouse down and think about it. As properly as individual pins on Pinterest, this is a great manner to examine whole Pinterest pin forums.

Consider whether or not or now not the fabric you're growing is evergreen as properly. Do you decided it has lasting power? Will it's as charming and exciting a yr—or maybe 5 years—from now while someone sees it for the number one time? Evergreen fabric is in no manner obsolete, and it remains applicable to Pinterest lovers 365 days after one year, no matter the season. You want to have a aggregate of topical, cutting-edge photographs and evergreen cloth so that it will continue to be applicable 12 months after one year to preserve your net website online on line searching clean.

Dissemination Techniques for Information

When it involves acquiring photos and movement images to your Pinterest forums, you have got a few one-of-a-kind alternatives to choose from:

Getting began on Pinterest is as smooth as repinning outstanding content cloth from different customers.

2.Pinning your very own particular records from a selection of diverse sources for your board

(These might likely embody different web web sites, blogs, and so on.)

three. It is vital to create your personal real Pinterest content material.

It's viable that every one three of these strategies will make primary contributions to your paintings. The companies and institutions that do the brilliant on Pinterest, rather, are regularly the ones who've the most particular content material material, this is described as pix that have now not been repinned via manner of the usage of every other Pinterest purchaser in advance than.

I've located that my very very very own content fabric is the maximum famous fabric on my internet website—that is, the subjects that different human beings repin and observation on the maximum regularly—and that that is right. Is this a correct declaration? The photos that grow to be well-known on Pinterest are people who I find out on special websites after which publish to Pinterest to get exposure (or create myself). Of path, to discover what works superb to your target market, you have to, of direction, behavior experiments that lets in you to discover what does.

According to facts, greater than eighty% of Pinterest content material is repinned from each different region within the Pinterest universe, because of this that you could come upon a big quantity of photographs that have been recycled. When it includes Pinterest, if you're already a consumer, you've got were given in all likelihood had the identical experience that I absolutely have: You're seeing the identical bunny photograph, outfit, or movie well-known person glam shot again and again another time to your Pinterest net page as the photograph makes its way throughout the internet and is often repinned with the resource of way of various individuals who are interested in it. If you are not presently a member of Pinterest, you want to simply maintain in mind signing up.

Examine the distinction among seeing the equal vintage image again and again once more and seeing a sparkling new photo that no person else has pinned—a few detail this is so precise that you have in no manner seen some aspect find it not possible to face up to in advance than—a few component this is so special from some factor else you've got got visible earlier than. The ability of learning some thing new, in addition to the possibility of being exposed to something new, are all topics that human beings are interested in. For Pinterest achievement, it is essential to preserve in thoughts how essential it is to find out particular pictures to pin.

Chapter 5: How To Make Your Website More Attractive To Pinners

As Pinterest keeps to boom in recognition, you may assure that increasingly more pinners may be scouring the internet for thrilling stuff to feature to their forums. Learn the way to optimize your blog articles and internet pages so that Pinterest visitors will revel in comfortable when they pin your fabric on this financial disaster.

Keep in thoughts that the more people who percentage your fabric on Pinterest, the greater web website site site visitors you'll get on your internet internet site on-line. For this motive, you ought to make each try to provide a heat welcome to anyone who visits your internet site on line via Pinterest. These smooth strategies will help you optimize your internet site or weblog for the Pinterest social media community.

Including Photographs in Your Website's Content

The first actual issue you should do to make your internet website greater Pinterest-pleasant is to consist of an photo (or severa snap shots) in each and every blog submit and web page that you submit for your internet internet site online. It's as easy as that: in case you placed up a weblog article without which incorporates a photo, it will now not be shared on Pinterest. When it comes to pinners, seen cloth is pinnacle! So if you locate yourself becoming slack about together with photographs for your posts, recollect that now not collectively with an photograph on your article way that no person will pin it.

Keep in mind that the extra visually attractive, attractive, or fascinating a photo is, the more likely it is to be shared and pinned. The photographs that enchantment to Pinterest customers are strong, expressive, and thrilling, that is some factor to preserve in mind at the identical time as selecting your pix for the internet site. The correct information is that attractive photographs paintings wonders to your everyday weblog readers as properly, so such as pics in your weblog articles will gain your blog web page site visitors as a whole. Everything from staff headshots to in the back of-the-scenes movement images to mindmaps and exceptional sorts of effective seen cloth that are shown in Chapter 6 are extremely good pix for blog posts.

The buy of stock pics for use in blog articles and web pages is also some component I advise. There are a number of inventory image net net websites from wherein you should buy super photographs and get royalty-free licenses with a purpose to will let you use such photos in weblog articles without attribution. Two of my preferred inventory image websites are iStockPhoto.Com and Shutterstock.Com. It's crucial to check the terms of issuer of the inventory image net internet site on line in advance than you use their pictures to your net web page or inspire your customers to apply them on Pinterest, even though.

The guidelines governing stock picture internet web sites are presently in flux. In the meantime, regardless of the truth that stock image corporations are certain to seize immediately to the power of Pinterest in the near future, it is an first rate concept to double-check together with your business enterprise of desire, just in case.

You need to moreover recall updating the pix on older weblog entries or going once more through your weblog information and such as pictures to any posts which have been previously published without photos. Remember that you in no way recognize whilst an antique weblog put up may also moreover get sizable momentum on Pinterest, so make certain that every archived article—even the ones which might be a few years antique—has a fascinating photograph related to it.

Home décor blogger Nester Smith (thenester.Com) determined the tough way that she desires to preserve an eye constant on her preceding blog posts—and that they will be a pretty normal (and worthwhile) supply of site visitors for her internet site. Smith's net website have become seeing a few surprising interest when she observed it in September 2011.

Affiliate income from an ebook she promotes on her website had extra than quadrupled in a matter variety of hours. It wasn't until she regarded into wherein all of the new purchases have been coming from that she determined that taken into consideration one in all her in advance weblog posts—one that have been published eighteen months earlier and that had a private tale in addition to a link to that e-book—had lengthy past famous on Pinterest. Pinners have been sending some of website online visitors to her internet site, which induced a upward thrust in ebook earnings as a end result.

Moreover, the web site site visitors persisted to go with the waft in. Users of Pinterest despatched 22,000 visits to the blog web web web page during the month of November 2011. And Smith's sales are persevering with to climb; in fact, income of that e-book thru her net website are truly exceeding $500 in step with month as of this writing.

As a end result of this text, consider to keep up along with your preceding blog postings. The international of Pinterest is whole of surprises, and also you in no way recognize at the same time as an antique article or net net page can be given new life.

Make use of hashtags to attract attention to your Pinterest profile.

Make certain to inform your website visitors which you've joined the Pinterest network after you've got created your Pinterest account and published some forums and pins. To draw hobby to the truth that you are a pinner, you can want to embody a large "Follow Me on Pinterest" button prominently on your internet site. The options to be had are either using the unfastened Pinterest button that Pinterest gives on their net net web site (see all the Pinterest sweets proper right here) or having your internet style fashion designer create a bespoke Pinterest button for you from scratch.

What is the proper area to place your Pinterest badge on your internet site? There are 3 key locations that I propose which you visit.

In the start, positioned your button in in reality certainly one of your blog or internet website online's skinny columns (sidebars) to get humans to peer it.

Incorporating the button into the format of your banner is step .

Incorporate links in your social media networks, which includes Facebook, Twitter, and YouTube, into your logo layout (as tested in Figure 7.1).

Remember that no matter wherein you choose out to place your Pinterest button on your internet site, it have to be it seems that glaringly visible to net web web page site visitors. Make it as clean as feasible on your site visitors to discover the link amongst your pins and forums that allows you to offer them with the best quantity of ease.

Bloggers who use WordPress need to pay close to hobby to the subsequent worries:

You're in fulfillment when you have a WordPress internet internet site on-line or blog which you host on your very personal server. You can use those awesome Pinterest plugins for WordPress to make your net web site even extra pin-friendly, and they are available freed from rate.

We've formerly included the basics of networking with unique Pinterest users in Chapter five. However, how are you going to start to construct a sturdy dating collectively collectively together with your Pinterest fans and fanatics in a manner that encourages them to reveal off unshakable aid in your brand? The subject rely of this financial disaster is obvious as day.

Customer manual on Pinterest is based cautiously on "whuffie," which Tara Hunt refers to as "whuffie." A e-book authored with the useful resource of Hunt, The Whuffie Factor, explains what she technique.

Reputation and cash are also factors that make a contribution to whuffie. A person's impressions of you're determined via their responses to you, their contributions to the network, and the way they see you. They might be brilliant or horrible. The weighting of your whuffie is relying for your contacts with agencies and those for your location. In my personal community, in which I've constructed a recognition for being useful, [my whuffie is higher] than it's miles in a present day community wherein I've in reality arrived.

Keeping in mind which you're gaining social foreign money via posting and tasty with others on Pinterest is critical. It's vital to keep a wholesome stability among promoting your very own content material material material and imparting connections to one of a type precious net web sites, system, and pix.

As in case your whuffie were a financial group account, you must deal with it as such: you need to deposit hundreds of cash on the manner to have sufficient coins to withdraw whilst you need it. You will rapidly run out of cash if you keep to withdraw cash at the rate of 1 withdrawal after any other.

Wuffie will not be created, and businesses on Pinterest that really pin links to their very very own net websites will now not upward push in reputation.

As a effect, their tries at pinning may be in useless. To be greater unique, the whuffie candy spot isn't decided while Pinterest users pin each promotional photos and unique types of cloth in the right quantity.

In the equal way that there's no mathematical components or set of pointers that ensures achievement on social media net net websites like Twitter or Facebook, there may be no approach for achievement on Pinterest. To advantage a extremely good enjoy of approaches a high-quality deal advertising and advertising is just too little, hold in thoughts the standards and tips from Chapter 3 and hold in mind your ideal customer. Put your self inside the feature of your brilliant purchaser even as searching at your forums. Think about it: there are masses of pins on Pinterest which might be truly classified ads, discounts, and one in every of a kind promotions. Do you need me to have a have a look at appealing photos, interesting facts, and motivational photos alternatively? Is there anything I'd be inquisitive about due to the truth makes me take shipping of as right with the author of the pin?

Your target market will increase to apprehend, like, and accept as actual with you on the equal time as you inspire self warranty to your customers and a whuffie in yourself.

On Pinterest, you can do a number of sports activities activities to decorate your social foreign exchange and decorate your dating together with your fanatics.

Don't be afraid to have a actual dialogue with humans you meet.

In preceding chapters, we referred to a number of strategies you'll in all likelihood connect with precise Pinterest customers. Check to appearance whether or not you're using those strategies effectively. In addition, you have to provide incredible articles on a month-to-month basis to the those who be part of your mailing listing due to your efforts on Pinterest. Neither you nor special corporations or groups must distribute unsolicited mail for your subscribers.

Be Receptive to Feedback.

Provide possibilities on your customers to percentage thoughts and offer comments about what you are doing on-line—on Pinterest, your internet website, and notable social media structures. Inquire approximately your organisation thru asking them questions which includes: "What do they prefer?" What exactly do they despise? What is probably completed to make their lives in this region a hint bit an awful lot less complex?

The question "What is your biggest query approximately social media/walking a weblog/content material cloth advertising and marketing?" has been the trouble of an entire lot of popular weblog posts. The solution has constantly been "What is your biggest question about content material fabric cloth advertising and advertising and marketing and advertising and marketing?"

One such article on Copyblogger had greater than 3 hundred replies! Keep in thoughts that your readers need to inform you what is on their minds and what's bothering them, so ask them. They want to be heard and understood.

Consider posting a comparable open submit on Pinterest when you have not already (or for your blog, with hyperlinks on your pins or forums). Inviting human beings to position up questions, inquiries, or urgent issues that will help you better understand what is going on with them allow you to better apprehend them. Even if you simply want to up the stakes a bit, you can usually offer a reward to 3 randomly decided on respondents, together with a 1/2 of of-hour of complimentary session or an less expensive unfastened gift. This can be a first-rate manner to get a few new customers and research greater about what human beings are having trouble with on the equal time.

After that, ensure that you employ the information that will help you amplify your business enterprise plan. Make use of it as concept for contemporary blog entries, Pinterest boards, new products, guides, and unfastened reviews, amongst one-of-a-type subjects. If your clients and capability customers assume that you understand what they are going thru and are doing everything you can to assist them, they'll purchase a few detail you located inside the market.

Accept and include the chaos.

When agencies launch blogs, Facebook pages, or Twitter debts, one of the vital anxieties they've got is that they may lose manage of the general public communicate. This is one of the most common fears organizations have. It scares them to keep in mind what others might say about them on their web websites and social media profiles.

There is simply no getting around that. You do, in masses of methods, lose manage of the discourse at some point of this device. But take into account this: whether or not you want it or not, human beings are talking approximately your corporation on the net. Is it more crucial that lets in you to be aware about one-of-a-kind people's feedback (each high-quality and lousy) so you can respond to them, or might you choose to located your palms on your ears and fake that nobody is speaking?

The thriller to being able to loosen up on social media is to simply accept and love the craziness of the environment. Pinterest and extraordinary social media structures are not approximately preserving whole control over each photograph, each statement, or every assertion at the internet. These agreements are in reality approximately handing up a few authority on your clients. Furthermore, it's miles really probable that humans will say subjects which you do not accept as true with. But, in case your customers have been to specific dissatisfaction with you, might now not you need if you want to address the difficulty immediately and reply? I'm positive I would probably!

If individuals have valid issues approximately your corporation that you are gaining knowledge of about on Pinterest, respond to them!

Respond to them, particular your regret for the mistake or problem, and inquire as to what you can do to assist rectify the scenario. Negative input have to not be disregarded! It is usually simplest to address the trouble straight away in place of pretending that there may be none.

Agility and flexibility are important functions for any corporation that desires to interact with its clients through social media. Now is the time to take a deep breath, loosen up your grip on the reins a bit, and get ready to experience the wild waves of the interactive net.

It may also make you enjoy higher about what you're doing in case your posts get extra interaction. Nothing is greater frustrating than liberating lots of extraordinary cloth and feeling like no person is analyzing it.

It's as if you're honestly shouting into the abyss on the identical time as you are listening. When other human beings make feedback and connect to you, it offers you even greater motivation to hold going!

Increasing the amount of Pinterest fans

You will find out that some of the standards in this ebook will clearly and organically help you in growing your following on Pinterest. Remember that the great of your Pinterest audience is a exquisite deal more important than the large shape of people that observe you. For people who want to be more energetic of their efforts to get extra fanatics, the following are 5 matters to recollect:

1. Follow certainly one of a type pinners' boards.This one may also seem honestly smooth, however it is in reality the fastest and maximum honest technique of growing a following. Many of the human beings you take a look at will return the preference, and your following will increase as a end result.

2. Pin usually.The style of people who repin, "like," and touch upon your fabric will boom as extra people discover it if you pin each day. As a result, set aside a hint quantity of time every day to perform a bit pining.

three. Look for (and pin) new and exciting content fabric cloth on a everyday basis.The greater modern you are, the more fans you could advantage; consequently, make the effort to find new items to pin (out of your net website on line and special internet sources) instead of actually reposting things you have already got.

5. Organize contests to inspire participation.Using this method all the time is

not some thing I advise, however it may provide a massive increase in your follow depend variety. Generally talking, I would like to look corporations growth their Pinterest followings extra slowly thru developing exquisite content, but the abnormal contest is OK.

Curation

Putting collectively a group of the satisfactory cloth for your venture and imparting it in an smooth-to-follow, nicely-prepared, and visually appealing manner is a superb way to look after your enthusiasts and provide them beneficial facts at the same time as additionally building their take delivery of as real with in you.

What is the definition of content fabric curation? In the terms of Beth Kanter, the founder of BethKanter.Org (@kanter), a social media representative for creative NGOs:

Organizing and offering fabric in a significant and based manner round a given problem is referred to as content cloth curation. It is the act of sifting through the large volumes of content material to be had at the internet.

Sifting, sorting, organizing, and publishing fabric are all a part of the task description. A content fabric curator selects the maximum huge and relevant quantities of content material cloth fabric to proportion with their intention marketplace with the aid of hand-choosing them from numerous property. It's exceptionally in assessment to the work a museum curator does to location up an exhibition: they outline the issue, they offer context, they decide which paintings to vicinity at the wall, how they want to be annotated, and the way they need to be exhibited for the general public to see them.

Content curation consists of deciding on the best records available on the internet—the most inspiring photographs, notion belongings, and thoughts—after which painstakingly organizing that content material material in a visually appealing manner for the advantage of your goal marketplace (your niche). When you are via reading, investigating, and accumulating facts, you are taking all the best bits of it and bundle deal them together especially on your readers and fanatics.

So, what does this need to do with Pinterest? The Pinterest version lets in you to collect organizations of fabric that can be prepared under any trouble you want, after which make lovable collages of your curated content cloth for others to experience, research from, and function a laugh with. You can create corporations of content material material that may be categorized underneath any concern count you select.

Pinterest can help you construct a lovely basis for a museum of your carefully selected mind and mind.

Different disciplines and sectors may have taken into consideration one in all a type sincere curators, and each board on Pinterest can also additionally characteristic a mini-collection of curated cloth in and of its non-public proper. In addition to being a former legal professional, Jodi Ettenberg (@jodiettenberg) is currently journeying (and consuming) her manner in the course of the globe. Jodi curates material about space on her great-cool Pinterest board titled "Space is Awesome," which she created. She has a Pinterest board committed to pictures of outer vicinity and the Northern Lights, in addition to photos of the celebrities and the moon. The last product is a visually terrific series of pix which might be each amusing to test and academic to have a look at from.

So, what types of forums may additionally you positioned up in your potential clients to look at?

Consider the subsequent situation: you personal an animal refuge and want to gather extraordinary message boards for cat, canine, and rabbit fanatics who are searching out the maximum up to date facts on their favored pets. There are a plethora of top notch canine schooling mind to be had, in addition to the finest belongings for building a rabbit hutch and the brilliant methods to maintain your cats entertained at the identical time as residing in a metropolis flat. By carefully and deliberately posting to the ones forums on a every day basis, your puppy-loving fans will begin to accept as true with you to offer them with the most reliable, updated, and nicely-vetted fabric at the issues that interest them.

By putting in the try to create remarkable statistics curation, you will set up yourself as a respected authority. In my opinion, there can be no higher way to growth your following than to take care of your Pinterest admirers on this way.

To conquer this tendency to assume in terms of character pins—and to stress over whether or not or not you need to pin a sure piece of material to a board to your company—consider your self because the sensible, present day, and discriminating curator of your non-public on line museum. Allow your network to are available in and endure in thoughts the high-quality of what you have got amassed for them; they'll be able to tell through the exceptional of the showcase which you located an entire lot of perception into placing every series together. Visitors to the museum are there to investigate from you, now not to be entertained. They need to take a harm from on the lookout for to filter out via the chronic attack of sparkling data to be had at the internet and find out what is crucial to them and their households (and what is not). They located their religion in you to tell them what the nice and most crucial bits of information in your area are at the time.

With Pinterest, you could do all of those objects, and you could open the door to a international wherein your potential to easy out and gather information have to make you a specially sought-after professional for your situation.

Robin Good, a blogger at www.Masternewmedia.Org, stated that content material cloth fabric curation may be very crucial.

If you stay in a worldwide wherein interest has turn out to be so scarce that it has become as precious as forex, and in which locating notable statistics on a particular problem remember calls for ever extra time and interest, the charge that [curation] can provide those who've the functionality to prepare, choose, convey collectively, and edit the maximum valuable records on any given subject count number is incomparably valuable. Curation is the capability to prepare, pick out, compile, and edit the maximum precious data on anyone subject matter, making it incomparably treasured.

Chapter 6: Who Uses Pinterest?

Understanding your target marketplace is vital for a a success advertising and advertising advertising marketing campaign. That is real for each social media marketing and advertising and conventional advertising. Whether you're focused on Pinterest with commercials or the use of the platform organically, you have to understand demographics and clients of the platform. It additionally allows to recognize the marketplace size.

NUMBER OF PINTEREST USERS

Pinterest had about 478 million monthly active clients by using using the zero.33 area of 2021, this is more than Twitter and different social networks. This tells you processes robust this social network is. Out of these customers, 50% stay out of doors america. Remember what I said about Pinterest utilization: it's far a international social network with customers from all walks of life.

Besides the us, Pinterest may be very active in Australia, Canada, the UK, Brazil, and Germany.

Pinterest has seen normal boom in its customers over time. The variety has been developing via tens of hundreds of thousands annually. This exponential increase comes as suitable information to any entrepreneurs concentrated on this platform. The desk below shows how the quantity of Pinterest clients has advanced through the years:

PINTEREST USERS BY AGE & GENDER

More than 60% of Pinterest customers are girl. This indicates that marketing woman-associated merchandise is greater powerful on Pinterest than distinct social media structures.

The median age of Pinterest clients is forty. However, those under 40 are the maximum lively pinners.

PINTEREST USERS BY INTENT

Another cause to advertise your products on Pinterest is the excessive style of customers seeking out buy inspirations. According to the Omnicore Agency, 89% of users are looking for purchase thoughts. With right pins about your product and optimized descriptions, your company will probable be extra visible on Pinterest and enhance income.

The following stats are of interest in case you need to excel in Pinterest marketing:

• Pinterest facts approximately 2 billion searches constant with month.

• 25% of virtual entrepreneurs use Pinterest—a signal that there may be a advertising and marketing possibility proper right here.

• 80 5% of energetic customers use the mobile app.

• 98% of lively pinners strive new mind and inspirations they locate on Pinterest.

• About 77% of weekly pinners have located a brand new emblem or product within the market.

• About 90% of weekly customers buy services and products primarily based on facts from Pinterest.

• Promotional pins are probably to growth leads by means of way of 60%.

- About 50% have completed their purchase after discovering a promoted pin.

For digital marketing and advertising and marketing managers, those stats are important at the same time as installing location a Pinterest advertising and advertising advertising campaign. They will help who to intention and the manner to do it. Most importantly, the stats show infinite opportunities to promote your logo, boom leads, and beautify profits, which can be the primary objectives of any advertising advertising campaign.

We have additionally seen how Pinterest affects looking for selections for its customers. Many clients exit of their manner to shop for a particular product in fact due to the truth they determined a pin on Pinterest about the product. They will be predisposed to remember that this platform gives the notable way to discover products, offerings, and mind they need.

WHAT IS PINTEREST MARKETING?

Now which you apprehend what Pinterest is and who uses it, it's time to get all of the manner all the way down to the actual business company: the advertising aspect of Pinterest. In this economic catastrophe, we're capable of discover about the subsequent:

• What is Pinterest advertising and advertising?

• What are the desires/functions of Pinterest advertising and marketing and advertising and marketing and advertising and marketing?

• How effective is Pinterest advertising?

DEFINITION OF PINTEREST MARKETING

Like all different forms of social media advertising and marketing, Pinterest marketing consists of formulating strategies and techniques to use the platform and create logo interest for your merchandise or business business enterprise. Through Pinterest advertising and marketing, you could expand your organisation. You will connect with many capacity consumers who spend their time on the platform.

With over 478 million active clients, Pinterest offers organizations and corporations high-quality outreach to customers. Pinterest customers are continuously exploring the platform for present day thoughts and inspirations, because of this you may display off your product and plant a seed in someone's thoughts in advance than they purchase your product or spend money on your emblem.

Pinterest advertising and marketing is finished thru the advent of pins which might be associated decrease returned to your net net website. For your pin to stand out amongst first rate pins within the niche, it desires to be visually appealing, self-descriptive, and make customers take movement. Viewers want to proper now understand the records inside the photo or video. We will communicate extra powerful Pinterest marketing and advertising in later chapters. So, preserve reading!

WHY IS PINTEREST MARKETING IMPORTANT?

Pinterest advertising and advertising and marketing serves the identical motive as every other social media marketing and advertising method. The first-rate distinction is that it is able to be greater effective right proper here than on exclusive structures.

In the previous financial smash, we checked out applicable crucial data that each Pinterest marketer want to recognize.

Here's a bit recap. Through Pinterest advertising and marketing, you may gain the subsequent:

• Create emblem attention by means of the usage of the use of accomplishing out to masses of lots of humans. You will boom your on line presence as your pins are seemed and shared.

• Drive site visitors for your internet website. Pins are backlinked to landing pages and generally redirect users on your net page whilst clicked.

• Increase leads and email subscriptions. With the advanced visitors for your internet internet website, you may get greater people to join up in your mailing list or buy your product.

HOW EFFECTIVE IS PINTEREST MARKETING?

Pinterest is dominated by using way of girl customers. But the considerable range of new male customers registering on the internet web page has been growing in modern-day years. Currently, the platform is turning into greater famous among GenZers (born among 1997 and 2012) due to the fact it's far a sea of idea and a place wherein customers can precise their creativity.

Many humans are already leveraging the power of Pinterest advertising. It is an incredible tool for backlinking to pressure web website online web site visitors to any net web site. In fact, it's far ranked first among social networks for having website traffic if you are strategic and create tremendous visuals.

Pinterest advertising is likewise powerful within the following techniques:

• Driving net web page web site site visitors: If you are on the lookout for traffic on your net net site, use notable visuals on Pinterest to get greater. Pinterest is one of the first-rate social media systems for steering web site visitors lower lower back on your net web page.

• Creating engagement: Pinterest is the marketplace chief in character engagement. Many active pinners are greater inclined to find and share pins with particular groups. It is a lot much less complicated to interact with influencers proper right here than everywhere else.

• Improving conversion: The conversion ratio of internet site online visitors from Pinterest is better as compared to wonderful channels.

• Discovering your target market: Unlike unique social networks, Pinterest allows you to research all about your target market the use of their analytic gear. Armed with the proper data, you could create pins for you to be shared by opportunities.

Pinterest can be an exceedingly effective advertising and marketing device, however simplest if it's used properly. In the following chapters, we are able to train you the manner to make the maximum out of this brilliant social media platform.

WHAT ARE PINTEREST ADS AND HOW WELL DO THEY WORK?

Pinterest marketing achievement relies upon on your capability to create pins and design classified ads which can be precise and stand out. Now which you apprehend what Pinterest marketing is and its efficacy, we're able to dive into Pinterest commercials. In this bankruptcy, I'll communicate the subsequent:

• What are Pinterest commercials?

• How do you set up a Pinterest ad?

• How do you manage Pinterest commercials?

• Who do Pinterest advertisements aim?

• How powerful are Pinterest commercials?

• Chapter recap

WHAT ARE PINTEREST ADS?

You can create a Pinterest pin and appearance in advance to it to organically seem in the search results or domestic feeds of your target market. But that technique can be slow and affects lots an awful lot much less customers. Pinterest has a feature called Pinterest Ads that lets in you to sell your pins.

Promoted pins emerge as Pinterest advertisements and characteristic more possibilities of appearing in are seeking for results for relevant searching for terms. This function is available for Pinterest commercial enterprise enterprise money owed to help them promote their pins. They may be pix, carousels, or motion photographs. In the near destiny, Pinterest might also even permit users placed up concept pins, which can be similar to Instagram reels.

Promoted advertisements are displayed each in are seeking effects for a given key time period or phrase and on the users' domestic feeds based on their preceding sports sports on the platform. Pinterest commercials can aim particular audiences based totally on the demographic information, hobby, and other elements you located at the same time as developing the ad.

TYPES OF PINTEREST ADS

There are notable forms of pins you can use while advertising and advertising and marketing and advertising with promoted pins. These embody the subsequent:

Static Ads

A static ad consists of simply one photograph in the recommended format of each .Png or .Jpeg. The most file duration and element ratio recommended with the useful resource of Pinterest are 20 MB, and 1000x1500 or 1000x2100, respectively. Any deviation from these limits can result in the picture being cropped on the equal time as rendering for viewing on home feeds.

Video Ads

These are movement images that pinners use to create brand

Awareness, display how-to's, or some thing else that calls for video presentation. The commonplace video codecs consist of .Mp4, .Mov and .M4v, and a maximum video duration of as lots as 2GB.

Pinterest video advertisements have a length between four seconds and 15 mins. The detail ratio advocated differs. They are:

• Standard width video commercials ought to be rectangular (1:1) or vertical (2:three or nine:sixteen).

• The maximum width of video classified ads should be 1:1 (square) or sixteen:9 (widescreen).

Like pictures in static classified ads, films in video classified ads also may be cropped or fail to play if the dimensions does no longer meet the necessities.

Carousel Ads

Carousel classified ads can be belief of as multiple static commercials combined into one. Instead of one image used inside the static classified ads, many snap shots are uploaded. Viewers can scroll from one to the subsequent with the aid of swiping at some point of the show or clicking the "subsequent" or "preceding" buttons.

2 to five .Png or .Jpeg snap shots are approved in step with carousel. The maximum document length is 32 MB with an thing ratio of one:1 or 2:3.

Shoppable or Buyable Ads

These are normally used Pinterest commercials for mother and father which are advertising and marketing their products. Shoppable commercials allow Pinterest customers to shop for whichever merchandise they decide upon proper at the platform without being directed to the advertiser's e-change preserve. You want to have your catalog in vicinity to create this form of ad.

Collection Ads

This type of advert has one huge picture and 3 wonderful smaller images describing the product. We can say it's miles a subset of Shoppable commercials. But in this case, you may want to installation Pinterest's feed ingestion tool (called the Catalog) before the usage of this ad kind.

SETTING UP A PINTEREST AD CAMPAIGN

You can set up a Pinterest ad advertising and marketing and advertising campaign in seven steps:

Step 1: Create a Business Account

You have options: changing a private account to a commercial organization account or developing a cutting-edge day enterprise account. You can select out to link this new commercial corporation account to the personal one if you want. I'll communicate a terrific deal more approximately this in the subsequent financial disaster.

Step 2: State Objectives of Your Ad Campaign

Every advertising advertising and marketing advertising campaign has an aim. Pinterest will spark off you to specify whether or not you want to create emblem attention, pressure website online site visitors, enhance income, and many others. And Pinterest will in shape up your ad with customers based in your objective.

The goal may additionally even decide the way you installation your bidding. In this case, "bidding" refers back to the bid your ad will make to Pinterest's set of tips to decide how immoderate you appear in are trying to find outcomes on Pinterest.

Step 3: Set the Budget

Setting a advertising and marketing campaign finances will maintain you on top of things of your rate variety. The advert will run for as long as you still have credit rating to your account. It stops once your price range are depleted. In putting the charge range, you may be required to specify the campaign budget kind, which you may set as every day or lifetime (in case you select lifetime, the marketing and advertising marketing campaign may be finished and your price range can be completed). Also, you can time table the advert to run constantly or on decided on days.

Step 4: Creating an Ad Group

An ad employer allows you to set up your advertisements with the useful aid of placing associated commercials beneath the identical advertising marketing campaign. Doing this additionally we can also want to Pinterest distribute your advertising and marketing advertising campaign price variety in a price-effective way. You can classify your ads constant with the goal market, interests, advert placements, and wonderful parameters.

You also can business enterprise an advert campaign based totally on demographic facts. For example, you may goal best girls below 35 years of age or an older populace of fifty and above. Pinterest will show the size of the target audience at the same time as you're putting in region your marketing campaign.

Step 5: Creating Your Audience

This step complements Step 4 via specifying greater parameters to correctly describe your target market. Choose what works for you and observe the activates.

You'll then be induced to feature an audience list, however that's optionally available and handiest advocated if you'd want to retarget your marketing campaign. Retargeting approach advertising to an goal marketplace that has already interacted in conjunction with your logo. This might also imply interplay with pin engagement, internet website online internet web page site visitors, or folks who introduced your product to their cart. Retargeting may be very powerful as people are much more likely to buy from you or undergo in mind your emblem in the event that they have interacted on the facet of your logo within the beyond.

Down the street, when your advertising advertising marketing campaign is more hooked up, Pinterest lets in you to pick individuals who take a look at you.

To higher seem in are searching for for results, you need to add relevant key phrases with sufficient are searching for volumes. Conduct specific key-phrase research to offer you with the satisfactory list an amazing manner to make your ad rank first (study more about key-word studies in financial disaster 8).

You moreover have the opportunity to perform demographic tuning. Here, you may aim your target market based totally totally on gender, age, region, language, or device. Choose all options that exercise to you.

Step 6: Creating the Ad

Select your pin for an ad. Then upload a key-phrase wealthy call and outline, a link to the website you would love your target market to go to, and a monitoring URL. Tracking URLs will assist you to look at man or woman classified ads with 0.33-birthday celebration tools like Google Analytics. If you only use Pinterest Analytics, you don't want to apply tracking URLs.

Step 7: Preview and Publish the Ad

In this final step, you can preview the advert facts after which placed up them if glad. It will usually take a pair hours on your ad to be accepted. Once posted, you can view the ad with the beneficial useful resource of clicking Ads at the top menu bar and then Reporting.

MANAGING PINTEREST ADS

The Pinterest Ad Manager is built right at the platform. You do not want any 0.33-celebration device to use it. With it, you could create new classified ads or manage gift ones via checking their reports and tracking the consequences to make crucial upgrades.

Every Pinterest ad is supposed to carry out constant together with your set desires. You have the potential to see why your ad isn't always behaving as anticipated and adjust it for that reason.

HOW EFFECTIVE ARE PINTEREST ADS?

Pinterest commercials or promoted pins have better possibilities of appearing on domestic feeds and in are seeking out outcomes of your aim clients due to the fact you have got such numerous options for targeted on and specifying your target market. Pinterest has emerged as one of the most powerful networks for advertising and marketing and advertising and marketing and advertising, growing emblem recognition, and in the end growing profits.

Pinterest, as a social network, is proving to be extra powerful every 12 months. Many clients sign in at the net page each day. Having a promoted pin approach your product is higher placed in advance than the goal marketplace.

Unlike the identical antique pins, you can determine who sees your advert. You may want to have higher conversion costs with promoted advertisements.

Step 1: Create a New Pinterest Account button.

Step 2: Scroll to the Bottom of the Prompt

At the cease of this show display screen, you will see a button that publicizes Create a free enterprise account. Click it to go to the following display display screen.

Step three: Fill inside the Form

The next display screen has a shape to fill to your non-public statistics, along with your e-mail, password, and age. Hit the Create Account button while you're finished.

Step four: Fill in Details for Your Business

The next display display screen will ask you for a business agency call, language, and region. Fill within the records and then circulate to the subsequent step.

Step five: Business Description

The subsequent prompt asks you to give an explanation for your industrial business enterprise. There are templates with statements. Just choose out the maximum appropriate solution after which click on on Next.

Step 6: Steps to Claim Your Website

a) Log in in your Pinterest Business Account. In the pinnacle right nook, click on on the drop-down menu and select Settings.

b) In the contemporary window that opens, click on Claim. This is decided at the menu panel at the left factor. That will will let you claim your net website.

c) Click the "Claim" button on the proper factor now to get right of entry to a pop-up as a way to assist you to claim your net website. There are three options: Upload an HTML report, Add an HTML tag, and Add a DNS TXT file on your area host.

Hover your mouse on the primary opportunity and click to duplicate the tag to your clipboard. After that, click on Continue.

d) Before you enter your internet internet page's URL here, you want to stick the HTML tag you copied from the previous step into the index.Html document of your net web web page. The technique for doing that relies upon on wherein your website is hosted. You can contact your net developer for information if you can't do it your self.

Open the index.Html file and paste the tag on the <name> phase, absolutely earlier than the <frame> segment. This will no longer have an effect on special tags you could have already got on that report.

Alternatively, you could declare your net web page through uploading an HTML document. To try this, click on the Download button to get the HTML document from Pinterest and then click on on the Continue button. Upload the currently downloaded file to the basis listing of your internet server. Once over again, you could contact your net developer for specific instructions to try this if you're not able to with your host internet web page.

e) The subsequent preference for claiming and verifying your net web page is to characteristic a DNS TXT file for your net internet site. Hover your mouse over the textual content and click on on on it to copy. Log into your DNS document and paste the TEXT into it. You may be required to characteristic an @ in the host document, which you need to do. After that, appearance in advance to the modifications to be performed in advance than you may circulate to the next step. This usually takes a couple of hours but can expand as lots as seventy hours.

The approach of pasting the Pinterest verification code to a WordPress internet site may be a chunk one among a kind. In that case, you can want to touch your internet developer crew if you are not tech-savvy.

Step 7: Provide Link and Finish Up

The remaining display will ask you to provide a link in your net web page. This must go to the homepage of your net internet site.

To finish installing and run your commercials, you can eventually want to install the Pinterest Tag. This can be finished manually when you have a WordPress, Squarespace, or custom net website online. If you've got a Shopify account, it'll in all likelihood be set up via Shopify's integration tool. For Etsy, there may be no manner to place inside the Pinterest Tag, however claiming your Etsy location may be sufficient in claiming all of the content fabric material on Pinterest that comes out of your Etsy keep.

Once you've completed all that, you have to be real to go! Your Pinterest commercial enterprise account is successfully installation and organized for pinning and strolling commercials.

CONVERTING A PRIVATE ACCOUNT INTO A BUSINESS ACCOUNT

Alternatively, you may convert an modern personal account right into a corporation account. To do so, log into your personal account and go to Settings. This is to be had as a drop-down menu at the pinnacle proper corner of the internet page.

On the settings net internet web page, scroll all of the manner down to account modifications and click on on converted account. That will take you to a ultra-modern net web page wherein you may fill for your enterprise agency account records as earlier than and whole the setup.

LINKING AN EXISTING ACCOUNT TO A NEW BUSINESS ACCOUNT

The very last opportunity is to link an existing account with a newly created industrial corporation account. To try this, log into your non-public Pinterest account, hover to the drop-down menu within the top right corner, after which pick out out Add account instead of convert account. On the trendy web page, pick out Create Business Account and look at the turns on to complete the setup.

Remember, converting a personal account will change your account to a enterprise agency account. If you need to preserve your personal account, then the ultimate choice I stated is right for you.

Chapter 7: How To Pin And Publish Content On Pinterest Like An Expert

In the following chapters, I'll educate you all of the tips and guidelines you need to achieve success on Pinterest as a marketer.

Your pins will decide whether or not you got the quantity of Pinterest advertising and marketing and marketing and advertising fulfillment you have been dreaming of. There are many marketers at the platform already. Here is how to beat the competition and stand out.

HOW TO CREATE A PINTEREST PIN

Pinterest customers are very active in terms of pinning. They pin logos, pics, icons, movement photographs, pictures, and additional. But in case you are going to use Pinterest advertising and marketing to beautify earnings, you've were given to do greater than truely pin. You need to be strategic.

Before going in addition, permit's learn how to create your first pin. With your Pinterest commercial enterprise company account created in the preceding bankruptcy, log in and keep as follows:

Navigate at the profile internet web page to a drop-down menu. From the drop-down menu that appears, click on Create Pin. A new show appears wherein you could upload extra information.

Adding Images or Videos

Upload an image or video of your preference. Then enter a destination hyperlink to a internet net web page (or anywhere you want people to be directed inside the occasion that they click on your pin).

You can upload an picture taken into consideration one in every of techniques. You can both upload an picture saved for your pc or mobile device or input the URL in which the photograph is hosted after which select out out the proper picture for you.

To perform the number one opportunity, click on on the gray container, in order to open the file explorer and allow you to select in which your picture is stored on the laptop. Wait till the image upload is whole, after which click Add a holiday spot link.

A new net page opens on the way to add a vacation spot link. If the photograph you want to pin is already hosted online, click on on Save from the internet internet web page (certainly under the gray photograph add discipline). Enter the internet internet site's URL, that allows you to be routinely linked on your pin as quick due to the fact the setup is complete.

You will see one or extra photographs lower decrease returned with the aid of Pinterest from the URL link you entered. Just scroll thru to locate the simplest you targeted.

Pin Title

Add a discover in your pin as quickly due to the fact the add is finished. Click Add your select out. The understand need to mirror the content material of the photograph and the content material on the touchdown web page in which the photograph is hosted. Titles want to be strategic and encompass relevant key terms so your pins are positioned by means of way of the right people.

ALT Text

You might also want to add ALT text for human beings with vision impairments so that it will percentage your pictures. And for video pins, you have to pick out cautioned categories related to your pin content cloth. Doing so will help Pinterest categorize your pin.

Pin Description

Add a pin description. A pin description discipline is just beneath the pin perceive and might hold as masses as 500 characters. The description is truncated to the primary 50 characters underneath the image whilst the pin seems on Pinterest Newsfeeds. For that reason, the primary 50 characters need to be charming and enriched with key phrases that growth the relevance of your pin. By relevance, I suggest it want to appeal to the right audience and be categorized effectively with the aid of Pinterest's set of rules.

Choose a Pinterest Board

Up till now, you likely did no longer have a board on your Pinterest enterprise account. That way you need to create a new one wherein your pins can be saved. Remember, your Pinterest boards help you put together Pinterest pins, similar to how files are used for grouping files.

If you have a board already that you need the pin to be stored to, pick out it and keep to the subsequent step. Otherwise, click on on Create board. Then call your board and give it an define. This newly created board will appear the subsequent time you create a modern pin. You will not should do it another time.

Choose whether or not or not to put up without delay or put up at a later date (you may time desk content material material up to fourteen days earlier). Then click on Publish to complete growing your pin. You're prepared! Now you handiest need to comply with the activates to make it move stay.

DIFFERENT PINNING FORMATS

Pinterest pins can be present day, video, or idea pins. Each has extraordinary uses and report formats, and Pinterest limits the record period, picture exceptional, and difficulty ratio.

Standard Pins

Standard pins are used for using website web site traffic in your net website online or e-alternate store through the provided hyperlink. If you're using Pinterest to decorate sales, then that is what you'll generally use. Standard pins have the subsequent specifications:

Video Pin

Video pins allow pinners to apply shifting snap shots to show a way, show steps, use a product, or show how a product appears from unique angles. With video pins, users who want extra facts approximately the video can get admission to it via the link provided for the pin. The vacation spot can be a internet internet site online or a social media account (I only advocate the usage of YouTube) in which the pinner has described the video in detail.

A video pin has the subsequent specs:

Idea Pin

You can think about a story or idea pin as a weblog publish. It is supposed to be informational. Idea pins allow you to add multiple snap shots or movement pictures that you can scroll via, and that they can help you encourage clients especially strategies than you will with everyday pins. Idea pins are a piece large than everyday pins, and they have the selection to feature "hobby tags," which will let you cause splendid audiences for your idea pin. The handiest hassle with concept pins is that you could't add a URL, which means that visitors received't be directed for your internet site. You CAN tag merchandise in concept pins even though, which makes them shoppable.

As I referred to, the rules for Story or Idea Pins are very extremely good from those of full-size pins or video pins, as noted inside the table below:

WHAT KIND OF SHOPPING FEATURES DOES PINTEREST OFFER?

Pinterest is continuously including new looking for abilities and updating their current-day competencies. So, now that I've defined the fundamentals of Pinterest advertising, permit's examine the only of a type buying competencies Pinterest has to offer:

Slideshow for Collections

Pinterest's "Slideshow for Collections" characteristic takes products from your catalog after which makes use of them to generate savvy series classified ads. It's a manner of making dynamic content material material tailored to precise customers, all of which takes region mechanically.

Merchant Details

This is every other new characteristic that lets in digital entrepreneurs on Pinterest to signify what their middle values are on their profiles. You can add facts together with "responsibly sourced," "invested in exceptional," "inclusive," "green," "Black-owned," "Latinx-owned," "Woman-owned," "LGBTQ+-owned," or "Disability-owned," on your profile.

These values can red meat up the connection amongst brands and their greater ethically worried target audiences on Pinterest. It additionally offers you the opportunity to get featured through using Pinterest as they're regularly highlighting brands with these middle values.

If you're inquisitive about including service provider information in your profile, you have to first test to the Verified Merchant Program on Pinterest, which I'll communicate subsequent.

Verified Merchant Program

Shopping scams have come to be commonplace on numerous social media apps through the years, foremost to many worrying or concerned customers. However, Pinterest presently created a feature to repair confidence among Pinterest customers as a way to revel in stable with what they're seeking out. This is called the Verified Merchant Program. The application showcases manufacturers that meet the minimum necessities of Pinterest's customer support and recommendations. Please keep in mind that the ones "minimum requirements" are not clean to hit.

These manufacturers are provided the "Verified" badge on their profiles. Getting the tested badge will installation extra take into account with buyers. It moreover allows for more perfect distribution on Pinterest and offers a metric reporting feature.

The software program started out inside the US however is now to be had in international places including Austria, Brazil, Italy, Mexico, the Netherlands, Spain, and Switzerland. The listing of to be had nations is developing swiftly.

Shopping List

The "Shopping List" is a extremely-contemporary characteristic on Pinterest that permits users to hold product pins and/or shoppable pins to a list. They can preserve viewing Idea Pins on Pinterest and pass once more to the shopping list later within the occasion that they need to buy something they've added to their list.

Shopping Lists are not available to all Pinterest debts but, however they're slowly rolling the feature out.

Shop Tab

Searching for products on Pinterest has now turn out to be easier than ever in advance than. You absolutely kind the product you're looking for into the hunt bar and then click the shop button. Doing so will show severa merchandise furnished on Pinterest which is probably associated with your are searching for.

This function changed into added as a right away stop end result of COVID-19. Pinterest sought to help corporations strength up their marketability after they had taken a profits hit from the pandemic.

Shopping From Boards

Pinterest now gives customers the selection to click on on on "Shop Board" on the same time as they will be browsing. This method that pins can now comprise product data, and clients can now maintain all the goods that a business organisation is promoting.

By selecting the "Shop Board" opportunity, they may see the products they can buy all pinned to the same board. These products will come from "Shoppable Pins" or as merchandise which may be tagged in pins.

Pinterest Catalog

Marketers can now use the Catalog function to add a list of all their products and create a storefront for them on Pinterest. The listed products can be sorted via the use of magnificence or product type for much less complicated discoverability. Also, you may promote them the utilization of buying advertisements.

With Pinterest's Catalog feature, your merchandise might be posted as pins automatically via Pinterest. These pins often gather big distribution from Pinterest, which means that they will get right of entry to wider audiences.

Camera Search

Pinterest now lets in clients to search for merchandise they desire clearly through using taking a photograph. The picture may be recognized thru Pinterest, and are seeking results will then seem for the person. If a client isn't proper with terms (possibly they're younger or communicate a distinctive language), that could be a top notch way for them to look for products. It's additionally super in case you see an object you want but don't have the choice to ask in which someone provided it.

Pinterest Tag

This function allows you to tune all conversions received from Pinterest onto your internet site.

Conversion Insights

The Conversion Insights metric helps you to apprehend what your excellent-performing pins are with regards to cart offers and sales.

Product Tagging

This characteristic lets you tag your merchandise on your pins so Pinterest clients can preserve for them right now from pins.

Rich Product Pin

This feature allows your product's inventory, charge, and any ability discounts to be displayed on the pins. You also can embody the product availability (supplied you use correct HTML tags). This characteristic is now handiest to be had for businesses with the Verified Merchant reputation.

MAKING PINS MORE ENGAGING AND CAPTIVATING

Everyone creates pins. To make yours stand out, they have to be engaging and fascinating. They must bypass beyond clean ordinary pins.

You want to learn how to flawlessly optimize your pins and cause them to fascinating to humans. They should make site visitors interested in know-how more approximately your merchandise. That is the handiest way you'll electricity extra visitors for your website and beautify earnings with Pinterest.

But how do you optimize your pins?

Use High-Quality Images

In the previous phase, I said the maximum image sizes and detail ratios that Pinterest accepts. Strive to get as near the limits as feasible. Using splendid images will supply data approximately its content material material fabric more in reality. Users are a ways more inclined to click on on on crystal-easy pictures in preference to blurred ones.

Also, you can make your pics extra colourful and delightful with photo improving. But if you aren't capable of developing such snap shots, you may surely preserve on with exceptional, inspirational, and informational snap shots which you locate.

Match Website Content with Pin Content

One of the worst errors Pinterest marketers devote is the use of their pins as bait. They trap people to go to a net website on-line that has amazing content material cloth from what the pin portrayed. Don't do this—it is going to seriously harm your ranking, therefore reducing your profits sales.

Always try to healthful the facts you provide on pins to the vacation spot internet site. The photo name and description offer a higher way of expressing the picture content material fabric near your internet internet site on line content material. They will also help your content fabric seem within the proper searching for outcomes.

Ensure Your Links Work

Without working hyperlinks, your Pinterest advertising and marketing may be fruitless. Pinterest will notice your hyperlink is damaged and they'll not push your content fabric material. When your pins bypass stay, check them your self to verify whether or not the hyperlinks are strolling.

Always Give Credit

It's smooth to scouse borrow content fabric cloth on Pinterest. People can pin or percentage other pins, however forget about approximately to credit score rating the owner.

If you are pinning other human beings's content material fabric cloth, keep in thoughts to offer them credit score score rating in the description with the resource of using their links. And to ensure you moreover may get credit score wherein you deserve it, embody your brand or hyperlink in all the photographs you add, because it's accurate for brand popularity. People who can be interacting with such photos on Pinterest will nevertheless apprehend wherein they got here from.

Use seek engine advertising-Rich Descriptions

Make use of the five hundred characters you are allowed to use to give an explanation for your pins. Perform key-word searches and use those terms even as describing your pins. Search for content or ideas associated with Pinterest-specific terms or key phrases, and if yours healthy, your pin will appear in the searching for effects. The same aspect takes vicinity at the same time as human beings are looking for mind on Google.

Use are searching for engine advertising-pleasant phrases precise to Pinterest to make your pins more visible and rank higher in search engines like google and yahoo like google and yahoo.

Add Call-to-Action Statement

Your pin has appeared on home feeds or in seek outcomes—amazing. Now the character viewing your pin is asking in advance to you to tell them what to do next. Without a name-to-motion statement, people are more likely to skip for your pin and find out the subsequent one. Use a applicable name-to-action on your pin and in your description to inspire site visitors to click to your pin.

Use Descriptions to Maximize Your Ideas

Pinterest pix need to be self-explanatory. It's no longer feasible to function all of the statistics you need your enthusiasts to apprehend pictorially, this is why we've the outline slot. Apart from the use of it to function key terms and provide an reason behind the picture in element, you can use it to give an reason behind your thoughts. Let human beings recognise all about your great thoughts.

USING RICH PINS

Rich pins include extra statistics like metadata embedded at the pin itself. This allows pinners to boom engagement. What you embody in a wealthy pin isn't associated with what's provided in the description. In truth, handiest the wealthy pin metadata can be seen at the same time as someone opens your wealthy pin as the description is probably overwritten.

There are 3 tremendous kinds of wealthy pins:

• Article pin: informs customers that the pin will lead them to the net web web page wherein the story is published. It typically contains the story pick out, author, and a pinnacle level view of the tale.

• Recipe pin: suggests first rate data approximately a recipe with out leaving Pinterest.

• App pin: displays a button for putting in the app with out leaving Pinterest. Unfortunately, best iOS is presently supported.

PINBOARD PLANNING

Planning or organizing your pins let you achieve more audiences that have pursuits specifically topics. Pinboard making plans sincerely way arranging pins through the usage of placing associated ones at the identical board. You have to no longer be blending topics. For example, you can have pins about your products. Here, you could create boards for kitchenware, apparel, shoes, and greater.

It's masses much less complex for people to view your pins in the event that they understand they could get everything they need in a unmarried vicinity. You also can produce other pins not related to merchandise. Say you moreover mght need to sell your weblog. You need to create a totally precise board to hold all pins associated with your weblog posts.

You also can aggregate attractive and inspirational pins with extra promotional ones at the same board. That is a smart manner of marketing and advertising and advertising your merchandise with out obviously telling your goal marketplace. As humans interact collectively together with your pins, they may get to recognize your product and emblem better.

Chapter 8: Utilizing Seek Engine Advertising Optimization And Link Building For Your Pinterest Marketing Gains

HOW TO MAKE YOUR PINS search engine optimization-FRIENDLY

Pinterest is like Google. People look for what they need the usage of terms or key terms. To make your pins discoverable, you need to optimize them. A properly-crafted pin has no price if clients cannot see it. Use the following seek engine advertising strategies to make your pins more seen on Pinterest:

Use Relevant Keywords inside the Title and Description

People discover pins via Pinterest searches. Some human beings will see your pins on their newsfeeds in case your pins are similar to something they previously interacted with. For this to art work, use the proper key terms in your pin discover and description.

Use key phrases with sufficient searching for quantity (greater about keyword research in the next financial ruin). Just like Google search engine optimization, avoid stuffing your key phrases. Use them sparingly and thoughtfully.

Create Captivating, Original Content

Create pins that humans want to view, repin, and interact with to beautify your are seeking engine marketing. Your pins must be applicable and hobby-grabbing. They have to be visually appealing and hold originality.

Create Video Pins

Users like sharing video content material cloth approximately things they love, inclusive of products, home décor mind, DIY tasks, and lots greater. However, Pinterest evaluates the relevancy of text plenty better than motion snap shots, which means movies are not great for using web page site visitors. Videos furthermore do no longer rank as excessive in search consequences.

Getting People to Pin Directly From Your Website

First, you want to assert your website (see monetary catastrophe five) and permit your rich pins. Doing so informs Pinterest that you are the owner of that website. Not best does that provide you with search engine advertising and marketing- ranking blessings, but it unlocks more analytic abilities of Pinterest. Pinterest gives precedence to pins created thru net internet web page proprietors because their authenticity is set up.

Now you can create new content material from your internet site.

But in advance than you try this, test what particular humans are already pinning approximately your internet site. Do that by using typing https://www.Pinterest.Ca/deliver/[yoursite] in the address bar of your browser.

Pin Regularly

Consistency is prime, and Pinterest rewards those who are everyday of their pinning. Instead of pinning , recollect weekly or monthly pinning and hold that over the years. Also, you can pin in the course of appropriate times at the same time as you assume your target marketplace to be online.

162

Save Pins on Relevant Boards

Saving your pins on applicable boards will purpose them to greater discoverable and decorate their ranking. Optimize your forums and use applicable keywords at the equal time as naming them.

Use Portrait Images for Pins

Pins with portrait snap shots are probably to rank higher because of the reality they have got better chances of showing on cellular gadgets. About eighty 5% of Pinterest customers (visit https://www.Masterful.Data/pin2 for brought records)get proper of access to the platform from their handset. You'll actually gain a larger target marketplace with vertical pics than horizontal ones. Consider an issue ratio of two:3 (which means an photo six hundred pixels large can be 900 pixels immoderate).

Optimize Your Profile

Don't simply reputation on pins at the same time as neglecting your profile. Your name and bio are what make you sincere on your site web site traffic. Use your actual name and upload a bio to explain who you're or what your commercial employer business enterprise does. Also, you could encompass applicable key phrases into your bio and nation the motive of your account to make you extra searchable within the are looking for bar.

MAKING YOUR DESCRIPTION search engine marketing-FRIENDLY

Using super snap shots or movies on your pins will appeal to people to it. A description will make humans choose whether or not or no longer they want to view greater of your content material cloth. Pinners use it to inform the target audience how treasured the pin is and encourage them to go to the net page. However, you need to be careful on the equal time as writing pin descriptions due to the fact they are with out troubles identified as direct mail.

But how do you are making your descriptions seek engine advertising and marketing-pleasant?

Use Keywords

To make your descriptions search engine advertising-first-rate, you want to start through using applicable key phrases that have a excellent are attempting to find volume. However, use them sparingly—you don't want your descriptions to come to be spammy and overrun with key phrases.

Also, don't use hashtags! Pinterest's set of regulations despises hashtags.

USE PINTEREST TO DRIVE MORE TRAFFIC TO YOUR WEBSITE

Pinterest one-manner hyperlinks will assist you growth traffic to your website online. The higher the visitors you have got, the more leads and earnings you can realise. You can build applicable oneway links for your website with the aid of doing the following:

Optimize Your Profile

Getting outstanding outbound clicks and vicinity traffic for your internet site calls for extra than virtually importing photographs/pins. You don't need your pins to get buried in a group of various pins like all of us else. The first step in optimizing your pins is gaining the consider of the audience. To do that, make sure your Pinterest profile is one hundred% entire. Consider doing the subsequent:

• Use a applicable username that resonates together together with your logo

• Complete the about section and add your bio

• Add region

• Upload a outstanding profile photograph— your logo can do

• Add a net web page link

Create Pinterest Boards to Organize Your Pins

Each pinboard company need to have a hard and rapid of applicable pins which might be visually appealing and informational.

Also, bear in thoughts developing collaborative boards where you can make a contribution together with unique organisation experts and influencers.

GET PEOPLE TO SAVE YOUR WEBSITE TO THEIR PINTEREST ACCOUNT

You also can grow your brand cognizance and decorate outreach via manner of allowing human beings to pin your content material. To gain this, you want to add a Save button to the photos in your WordPress or Squarespace internet web web page.

By together with the Pinterest Save button to the pictures for your net website, Pinterest clients can with out issues pin them on their profiles. So, how will you do it? Here are a few smooth steps.

Adding a Pinterest Save Button to a Squarespace net internet web page

First, log into your Squarespace account. Next, click on the Marketing button at the number one panel.

Choose Pinterest Save Buttons next. Then create the pin button format and pick out wherein you want it to be visible in your internet site. This can be on blog posts, product pages, or every.

Adding a Pinterest Save Button to Shopify

As you probably did with the Squarespace internet internet page, you could furthermore upload Pinterest Tags or save buttons for your Shopify product pages. However, the method is

167

extended and may require a level of statistics the usage of the Shopify dashboard.

Refer to (https://www.Masterful.Info/pin5) for particular steps.

Adding Pinterest "Pin It" Button to a WordPress Website

Similar to Shopify, you may want in advance understanding of using WordPress to installation "Pin It" buttons on your internet site. It takes time, however it's truly well worth it.

You can upload the button using widgets, concern topics, or jQuery. It's also possible to create a floating button. Use any of the four strategies of making the Pinterest button stated at (https://www.Masterful.Info/pin6) to set this up.

FINDING KEYWORDS AND TOPICS ON PINTEREST

When carrying out Pinterest key-word studies, you should keep your eyes on the are

168

attempting to find volumes and competition diploma. These metrics will help you understand how your pins and forums will carry out whilst the important thing phrases are efficaciously used.

Pinterest key terms variety from desired keywords utilized by different search engines like google like Google. They may want to probable have the same metrics, however their are searching for volumes and opposition degree are specific. That's due to the reality Pinterest uses excellent standards to rank pins and forums. I'll talk this greater in this financial spoil.

After conducting a hit key-word research, you need to realize wherein and a manner to apply your key terms. You can use them on your business corporation call, profile, board titles and descriptions, pin name and descriptions, picture record names, and within the URL of the link provided for the touchdown web web page. Keywords have to be used sensibly with out spamming the visitors. When you use them, ensure your statements are logical, smooth, and regular with key phrases.

To without issues navigate this chapter, we've got were given divided it into the following subsections:

• General Keyword vs. Pinterest Keywords

• Competition Level and Search Volume

• Pinterest Keyword Tool

• Other Tools for Finding Keywords and Topics

• Additional Keyword Strategies

Keep studying to discover the whole lot you need to understand about Pinterest key terms.

GENERAL KEYWORD VS. PINTEREST KEYWORDS

First, you should recognize the distinction a number of the utilization of key terms on Google and on Pinterest. Different search engines like google feature in particular techniques. Allow me to provide an cause of.

Words Searched on Pinterest Are Not the Same as Words Searched on Google or Other Search Engines

If you want to electricity traffic or create logo reputation on Pinterest, you need to use Pinterest-particular key phrases.

The identical is actual for sizable key phrases on Google and special serps. If you want to rank better on the ones systems, undergo in mind the use of those desired key terms. These may be determined the use of gear which encompass Google Keyword Planner (when you have a Google AdWords advertising and marketing advertising and marketing campaign).

Most key terms on Pinterest are related to thoughts. Many people turn to Pinterest to get concept from special pins and borrow or proportion thoughts. That isn't always the case in relation to Google and remarkable serps. We all recognise that people look for some thing and the whole lot under the sun.

Pinterest Displays Pins and Boards Without Users Searching for Them, Unlike Google

If you create integrative, attractive, and applicable pins, they'll appear on home feeds. Unlike on Google, you don't need to kind some thing within the Pinterest search bar to view content. However, you ought to be logged in to view content cloth related to your profile. The standards used to show content cloth on domestic feeds consists of profile authority, content fabric remarkable, and relevance associated with the pastimes and conduct of Pinterest customers.

If you need your content material to appear on the top of Pinterest seek consequences, do not depend best on keywords. Ensure your pins are creative and tasty, cowl 12 months-to-year trending subjects, and ensure they will be perfectly organized on nicely-defined boards.

PINTEREST KEYWORD METRICS: COMPETITION LEVEL AND SEARCH VOLUME

Before persevering with, permit me in short provide an reason for the distinction a few of the ones vital key-phrase metrics.

What is Keyword Research Volume?

Keyword Research Volume (KRV) refers back to the sort of seek queries recorded for a particular keyword in a given time body. In different phrases, it represents the amount of those who typed the word or phrase on Pinterest.

To find out key-word research volume statistics, you should use the Pinterest Trend tool. Here is the link to the device: (https://traits.Pinterest.Com/).

What is Keyword Competition Level?

Keyword opposition diploma refers to how difficult it is to rank appreciably on search engines like google like google and yahoo for a specific key-phrase. The higher the competition stage, the more difficult it is to gain an notable ranking for that key-phrase.

What is the Recommended Keyword Competition Level?

You need to no longer goal quite aggressive key terms because of the reality it's miles almost not possible to overcome incredibly set up profiles that use them. Also, going for low opposition key phrases isn't a super concept within the event that they have low are looking for volumes. Fewer humans seeking out key phrases equals fewer impressions and engagement on your pins. That approach you can gather plenty less powerful alerts from Pinterest, which leads to lower authority and worse ratings.

So, what is the encouraged key-phrase opposition degree to recollect on the identical time as analyzing Pinterest key phrases? Well, it's not viable to country a specific price for this because of the fact the competition degree varies for particular key phrases and industries. As a rule of thumb, cause keywords with slight competition or low competition but with slight or immoderate seek volumes. Only intention low-opposition key phrases in the event that they have got a excessive enough are trying to find quantity.

PINTEREST KEYWORD RESEARCH TOOLS

There are many elegant keyword research equipment, but I will best communicate about what can help you on Pinterest:

Pinterest Keyword Tool

The Pinterest key-word device is the number one device you ought to keep in mind the usage of to enhance your ranking at the platform. It is to be had with out value to all Pinterest registered individuals and has an smooth-to-use interface. You do now not want any earlier information to use it for key-word studies. It will provide you with get right of entry to to key terms used within the course of the whole internet site.

How to Access the Pinterest Keyword Tool

There are strategies of having access to the Pinterest key-phrase device: Pinterest searching for bar and Pinterest Keyword Planner through Pinterest commercials. Log in on your account and click on on on at the are looking for button to deliver the search bar into reputation.

Without typing a word, you will see the most popular key-phrase recommendations highlighted beneath it. The seek bar is at the whole used to find out long-tailed key phrases or key phrases related to your recognition keyword. The advised phrases is probably proven as you type a word within the are seeking out bar. Entering the important thing-word "Pinterest advertising" resulted in this:

Accessing a key-word planner is a bit hard because of the reality it's miles hidden with the useful resource of default. To use it, you need a Pinterest employer account. Refer to the previous chapters to learn how to create a new commercial enterprise business enterprise account or convert an modern-day non-public account. Once completed, proceed with the following steps:

Step 1: Accessing Pinterest Ads

Log directly to Pinterest Ads (https://ads.Pinterest.Com/) and click on the drop-down Ads menu. Please word that Pinterest Ads are supported in a few international locations satisfactory. If your usa is not supported, you want to pick a awesome u.S.A. From the speak area that pops up.

Click Create ad at the drop-down menu.

Step 2: Creating a Campaign Name

After clicking Create Ad, the above display appears. Here, you need to create a pseudo campaign call and go away all unique fields easy. Type some thing and click at the Continue button at the bottom of the internet web page.

Step three: Typing a Keyword to Get More Related Keywords

On the modern day internet page that looks, scroll all the manner right all the way down to the key-word segment. To free up this section, pick out Find new clients within the Targeting statistics phase:

Expand the Interests & Keywords segment through way of clicking the drop-down menu on the proper facet:

Click Add keywords and sort your seed key phrases. Pinterest key-phrase planner will at once show suggestions and are looking for volumes. For instance, getting into the important thing-phrase "advertising and advertising and marketing mind" again the following consequences:

When you are becoming ready your advert, you could also set your target audience primarily based on demographics. Here, select desired gender, age, place, language, and gadgets to be extra precise at the side of your advert and key-phrase searching for.

How to Conduct Pinterest Keyword Research Using the Tool

Now that we apprehend a manner to access the device, it will not be difficult to apply it.

On the hunt bar within the key-word phase, type a seed key-word (a quick-tailed key-phrase, typically one or terms, with excessive monthly seek quantity and competition). For example, typing "garden decor concept" back the following outcomes:

178

There is a scroll bar at the right aspect of the quest result location. You can scroll all the way proper all of the manner right down to view greater effects of your seek. Remember, you don't want key phrases with the very terrific are attempting to find volumes due to the fact the ones are frequently very competitive.

Assuming we are engaging in key-word research for the phrase "Pinterest marketing and marketing," we're able to realise the capability target audience length of any associated keyword. Just select out any phrase from the listing and paste it within the vicinity on the left thing. The goal market length is probably established inside the challenge at the top proper nook of the display.

You can find as many key phrases as possible to use on your Pinterest commercials, pins, and forums. Save your findings in a superb record—preferably an Excel spreadsheet or a Google spreadsheet—for reference and to avoid losing them.

USING THE TRENDS TOOL ON PINTEREST

Thus a long manner, I've established you a way to apply the Pinterest Guided Search Tool to discover trending key phrases or key terms related to your product. However, there may be a few other, extra moderen tool that allows you to look how specific phrases style at a few level inside the 12 months. Here, I'm referring to the Pinterest Trends feature.

What is the Pinterest Trends Tool and How Do You Access It?

As the decision suggests, the Pinterest Trends function lets in you to conduct key-word studies through studying how a given key-phrase has finished through the years. You can music a phrase's are seeking volume over the last 360 days.

Currently, Pinterest Trends is available for clients within the United States, Canada, and the United Kingdom. However, are looking for requirements and/or outcomes within the UK are usually relevant to maximum one among a kind global places in Europe as they generally observe the equal traits.

To get right of entry to this option as a US resident, really log into your Pinterest Business account. Click the drop-down menu subsequent to the Analytics tab, then click on Trends.

Those who live within the UK or Canada can also get right of get entry to to the Pinterest Trends tool thru (https://dispositions.Pinterest.Com/). Clicking the hyperlink will take you right away to your account, but only in case you are within the noted america. Otherwise, you'll get an errors that looks as if the screenshot demonstrated beneath.

How to Use Pinterest Trends

First, complete the steps I sincerely noted above to get proper of get admission to to the Trends segment. Second, type a seed key-word in the search bar. Suggestions will automatically pop up.

Select your chosen key-word thru clicking on it. Then you'll be capable of view how it's trended within the beyond 360 days. Specific phrases can hit a pinnacle are trying to find quantity throughout one-of-a-type times, weeks, or months of the three hundred and sixty five days. This may be represented on a graph from a scale of 1-one hundred.

Pinterest Trends might also listing different associated phrases to the simplest you've truly searched. You can click on on on on any of these associated key terms to look the manner it has trended at some level inside the beyond 12 months.

The final element of the Pinterest Trends device I'd like to say is the famous pins section on the very stop of the net page. Here, pins which might be relevant to chose phrases are proven. If you've determined on multiple time period, the graphs may be coloured in a certainly one of a kind way, and the associated pin list may want to have the equal shades to differentiate them.

Why is Pinterest Trends Essential for Marketing on Pinterest?

Pinterest Trends facilitates making a decision the precise key terms to encompass inside the call and outlines of your pins. But how does it range from one in every of a type key-word gear?

First, Pinterest Trends is mainly for analyzing trending terms on Pinterest. That approach you can collect your meant intention market at the platform. And 2nd, you're given a graphical view of approaches words were used for the past three hundred and sixty five days on Pinterest. This will assist you apprehend whether or no longer key terms you want to use are relevant/trending or now not, and therefore whether or no longer you need to be using them.

TAILWIND

Tailwind is a Pinterest and Instagram advertising and marketing toolkit that lets in bloggers, e-alternate personnel, and companies of all styles and sizes. It permits you to time table social media posts on the tremendous times, create cute pins and images faster than ever, discover a tremendous form of content material, make bigger your outreach, and diploma all types of metrics and analytics multi function region.

Tailwind will prevent hundreds of time. Let's dig in to see the way it definitely works.

How Tailwind Improves Your Profile Authority on Pinterest

Tailwind can assist improve your Pinterest presence in masses of tactics. Here are some matters you could do the usage of the software:

• With Tailwind, you may frequently pin without logging into your Pinterest account.

• Carefully time desk your posts definitely so they don't appear suspicious to Pinterest or your modern-day lovers. Your pins will located up frequently, as a quit result enhancing engagement with customers.

• Tailwind determines the high-quality time to place up your pins. This saves you the time of doing the equal manually.